*Motor development in
early childhood*

A GUIDE FOR MOVEMENT EDUCATION
WITH AGES 2 TO 6

A child is a child
wherever he may be.
But a child
is a child
only once . . .
And some say
that if he is not a child
who is helped to grow,
then he may not be
the adult
he could have been . . .[1]

[1]*Time for Learning,* National Focus on Early Childhood Reading,
Newsreport, Vol. II, No. 7, May-June, 1968.

Motor development in early childhood

A GUIDE FOR MOVEMENT EDUCATION
WITH AGES 2 TO 6

Betty M. Flinchum, Ph.D.

Professor of Education, University of North Florida,
Jacksonville, Florida

with 143 illustrations

The C. V. Mosby Company

Saint Louis   1975

Library of Congress Cataloging in Publication Data

Flinchum, Betty M   1934-
   Motor development in early childhood.

    1. Perceptual-motor learning. 2. Child study.
3. Education, Preschool. I. Title.
[DNLM: 1. Motor skills—In infancy and childhood.
2. Movement—In infancy and childhood. 3. Physical
education and training—In infancy and childhood.
WE103 F622m]
BF723.M6F55   372.8′6   74-13129
ISBN 0-8016-1587-9

VH/VH/VH   9   8   7   6   5   4   3   2   1

Preface

The critical nature of the teacher's ability to deal with perceptual-motor skills has received continually increased attention in the literature on early childhood. Many innovative educators believe that early exposure to planned motor skill learning will enhance the child's educational readiness and intellectual potential. In addition, there are some societal and cultural pressures for mass early childhood educational systems throughout the country. Predictions indicate that 40 percent of our preschool-age children will be involved in public kindergarten programs by the fall of 1975. This will necessitate a large increase in the demand for trained personnel to work with young children to provide meaningful programs for millions of children of all socioeconomic levels from eighteen months to five years of age.

The recent White House Conference Report stresses programs in early childhood that accelerate a "healthy sense of identity" in today's world. The conference cited inadequately trained personnel in nurseries, day-care centers, kindergartens, and child development centers as a major obstacle to the emergence of healthy identities. The White House Conference also stated that movement can be a prime motivating force for young children and can offer opportunities for exploration and achievement. White's study on the concept of competence establishes motility as a drive in its own right, and states that feelings of competence are dependent, in part, on opportunities for movement exploration. White, a clinical psychologist, believes that motility emerges between ten and eighteen months and causes a radical change in a child's world. He urges mothers to fill their child's world with objects that encourage movement.

Movement plays a very important part in the development of the young child. Movement activities provide a joy to the young child as well as the potential for use as a learning modality.

Child development specialists, day-care center directors, kindergarten teachers, physical educators, perceptual motor specialists, and others who deal with young children have become increasingly aware of the usefulness of movement or play activities in the education of the child. Many of these educators are including movement education activities in the daily learning curriculum for the young child.

This book has been designed to offer a program of motor activities for the teacher of the young child with objectives, ideas, content activities, strategies, equipment suggestions, and evaluative measures for working with the young child through a movement medium. It also includes a knowledge base for observing and analyzing the movements of children through a basic taxonomy of fine and gross motor skills and a pictorial analysis of selected skills.

This book has been written for use in professional preparation courses in a variety of disciplines. It may be used in early childhood courses where the young child's motor development and early childhood educational techniques are being studied. Child development specialists and physical educators will be able to utilize this text in early childhood and elementary movement education courses. It can also serve as a discourse guide for all persons who are working in the motor development areas with young children.

The text is organized to offer knowledge in four areas. The first area deals with the basic motor development and readiness of the young child for movement activities. It reviews the basic literature on motor development in early childhood and cites the relevant research concerned with children's motor skills. The latter part of this discussion offers selected learning strategies for observing and analyzing motor development.

The second area explores the learning and developmental theories commonly used in early childhood education. The theories are related to movement education activities with concurrent environmental stimuli and motility equipment.

The third area offers the instructional approaches for using movement as a learning modality. Teaching strategies and classroom management techniques are given along with activities for concept formation utilizing movement as the instructional tool.

The last area concerns general educational implications which can be ascertained from motor activities and movement learning. Educational motivations are suggested.

I would like to extend grateful appreciation to the Director, Nina Bennett, and to the staff of the Presbyterian Church of the Way Children's Center, Baton Rouge, Louisiana, for allowing the research in Chapter 3 to be conducted at the center. Appreciation is also expressed to Mary Louise Life, Louisiana State University, who assisted with the study, to the children who served as subjects, and to their parents for their permission and cooperation. Gratitude is expressed to Sharon Church for the illustrations, and to Marjorie Sunby for typing the manuscript. I would also like to acknowledge the helpful assistance of the Health and Physical Education faculty and students at the University of North Florida in the development of the book. Special recognition and thanks should be given to Margie R. Hanson, Elementary Education Consultant, AAHPER, Washington, D. C., for her contributions to the motor development curricula in early childhood programs throughout the country and in national organizations, and to Elsa Schneider, USOE, Washington, D. C., for her many contributions to the health and physical education programs for young children throughout the world.

Betty M. Flinchum

Contents

Motor development in early childhood

A GUIDE FOR MOVEMENT EDUCATION
WITH AGES 2 TO 6

If you want to know what a child is,
study his play; if you want to affect what he
will be, direct the form of play.[1]

chapter 1

Children and movement

The preschool child is a dynamic individual with spontaneous inquisitiveness and multiple physical abilities. Motor skills are his special tools for experimenting and expanding his environment. Play is his form of communication and learning. Movement or motor activities are so much a part of the preschool child's life that they should be given major consideration in understanding or determining his aptitudes and capabilities. A well-known early childhood specialist, Hymes, wrote that, "The day will soon come when all young children will have the chance to begin their schooling in 'first grades' and the first grade will be for three-year-olds to third grade. Gone will be the special names: nursery school, kindergarten, day care."[2]

It was reported by the National Commission on Teacher Education and Professional Standards that if present trends continue, 40 percent of the 3- to 5-year olds will be in school by 1975. If public kindergarten is made compulsory, and if voluntary programs are provided for 3- and 4-year olds, the school enrollment of 3- to 5-year olds will increase by over five million by 1975.[3]

Focus is being given to the preschool-age child in many ways. A television series for preschool children was launched in 1969 and continues to receive wide support. It was initiated by National Educational Television, The Carnegie Corporation, the Ford Foundation, The Office of Economic Opportunity, and The United States Office of Education, which created a

Children's Television Workshop (now Sesame Street) to develop a series of programs for 3- to 5-year olds that would not only entertain them, but would teach them as well. The aim of the Children's Television Workshop was to create a program series that would first capture young hearts and minds as thoroughly as the television commercial has and then would teach them such basics as the alphabet, numbers, time and space concepts, and problem-solving skills.

Pace, repetition, and combinations of live-action film and animation were among the elements tested for success in selling preschoolers. In addition to the program, a monthly parent-teacher guide was prepared that listed the elements of each day's lesson and follow-up activities and games for children to reinforce what they had learned.[4]

Articles in various magazines have offered information for parents for the development of the preschool child. Excerpts from Pines' book, *Revolution in Learning: The Years from One to Six,* were printed in McCall's Magazine. Pines reported that psychologists believe a child's future depends most on what he learns before the age of 6.[5]

Bonnie Prudden has published messages to be "fit by five," encouraging parents to set up exercise classes for the "diaper set." Her belief is that "since experts tell us that the lifetime pattern for physical development, like I.Q., is cast by the time a child shoves off for kindergarten, parents can't waste the early years."[6]

While this current interest is encouraging for educators of preschool children, the fact remains that very few studies have been done with the preschool child. Halverson said that "seldom in history has more attention been given to the importance of motor experience in the total development of the preschool and elementary child."[7]

She stated further that diverse educational fields are agreeing on the importance of early motor activities in the life of the child, and that physical educators are improving the programs for young children (Fig. 1-1).

Halverson felt that even with all this recent interest and attention focused on the young child, many assumptions about child development are still based on research of the 1930s, very little of which was contributed by physical educators. Research in the motor development area probably was game- and activity-centered from 1930 to 1960. During that period skills were the most important consideration, since they contributed to success in games. Most of the subject content centered on games and dances for children. Methods of skill development were neglected, and often teaching suggestions were inaccurate or misleading.[8]

Fig. 1-1

There is currently a trend to educate younger and younger children. Kindergartens, Head Start programs, parent-child centers, day care centers, children's universities, and other forms of preschool education are widespread. Structured nursery schools are prevalent for 3-year olds and many educators feel that these systems may be reaching children during the most important years. The scholar of human movement and perception might have more to contribute to the very young child than many other professionals.

Cratty stated that studies are needed on the movement capabilities of young children. He listed the emergence of motor patterns in young children as one of the areas that he considers to be in the most need of study and practice.[9]

Fig. 1-2

Several child development specialists support the reasons for providing motor learning experiences for young children and why they would be beneficial. Carpenter stated, "Not much is known about what activities stimulate the educational development of a child, but it is probable that the responses to the physical educational activities constitute their full share."[10] (Fig. 1-2.)

It has been acknowledged that physical abilities and skills contribute to self-concept and to an ultimate role in life. In support of this theory Horace English stated that in our culture a child's physical vigor and his ability in games and sports are likely to influence markedly his attitude toward himself.[11] (Fig. 1-3.)

And Jersild, another leading child psychologist, stated that, in his

Fig. 1-3

Fig. 1-3, cont'd

opinion, throughout life a person's view of himself is influenced by his perception of his body and its properties, his strength, and his skill in physical activities.[12]

REFERENCES

1. Gulick, Luther: Philosophy of play, New York, 1920, Charles Scribner's Sons, p. v.
2. Hymes, James L., Jr.: Teaching the child under six, Columbus, Ohio, 1968. Charles E. Merrill Publishing Co., p. 3.
3. National Commission on Teacher Education and Professional Standards: Preliminary report of the AD HOC joint committee on the preparation of nursery and kindergarten teachers, Washington, D. C., 1968, National Education Association, pp. 1-4.
4. Sesame street, Saturday Review, November 15, 1964, p. 91.
5. Pines, Maya: Revolution in learning; the years from one to six, New York, 1967, Harper & Row, Publishers, p. 21. Cited in McCall's Magazine, May, 1968, p. 74.

6. Segal, Jo Ahern: Fit by five, Look, April 7, 1970, pp. 76-78.
7. Halverson, Lolas E.: The development of motor patterns in young children, Quest **6:**44, 1969.
8. Halverson, p. 45.
9. Cratty, Bryant J.: Perceptual-motor behavior and educational process, Springfield, Ill., 1969, Charles C Thomas, Publisher, p. 65.
10. Carpenter, Ailene: Tests of motor educability, Child development **9:**293, 1940.
11. English, Horace B.: Dynamics of child development, New York, 1961, Holt, Rinehart & Winston, Inc., p. 256.
12. Jersild, Arthur T.: Child psychology, Englewood Cliffs, N. J., 1960, Prentice-Hall, Inc. p. 60.

chapter 2

Movement activity in children

The review of pertinent literature will be presented in three categories; cinematographic studies for the assessment of motor skills in children, child growth and development studies of motor patterns, and perceptual-motor studies with implications for young children.

THE ASSESSMENT OF MOTOR SKILLS IN CHILDREN

Cinematographic assessment for measurement in genetic movement patterns has been used in current studies. A review of literature relating to the knowledge of growth, child development, and motor learning will indicate these trends in studies with young children (Fig. 2-1).

Sinclair conducted a 3-year longitudinal study to determine the progressive growth in movement and movement patterns of children 2 through 6 years of age. Ten characteristics were identified; opposition, dynamic balance, total body assembly for speed, effective use of body parts in power release, total body assembly for utilization of the summed strength of several body parts, simple rhythmic step patterns, cross laterality, alternating use of the legs in a foot action, eye-hand efficiency, and posture alignment.

Findings included portrayal of developing patterns of a normal child, ages 2 through 6 years, a portrayal of sequential development of each fundamental movement through early childhood, an estimate of derivation of movement patterns within the normal range, identification of some de-

Fig. 2-1

viation that indicated a need for attention and for remedial measure, and case studies that would be helpful in showing how characteristics change or persist and how certain factors appeared to be related.[1]

Since 1962 Halverson has been conducting a longitudinal cinematographic study of preschool children of ages 4 through 6 years. The purpose of the study was to observe developmental changes in selected motor patterns of preschool children. The major study emphasis was on throwing in the overarm pattern, striking with the sidearm and two-hand pattern, punting and place kicking, the broad jump, and catching patterns.

Filming and audio taping observation records were gathered for three boys and three girls from ages 3 through 9. Records for each child were taken at 3-month intervals through ages 3 and 4; at 6-month intervals through ages 6 and 7; and were planned for yearly intervals through 8 and 9.

The film records of the motor performances were taken with a 16-mm movie camera. A tape recorder was used to obtain verbal interaction. The data were studied through film tracings, prints of motion picture frames, and transcriptions of filming session tapes. No conclusions have been reported since the study is still in progress.[2]

Deach conducted an important study on the motor skills of children 2 through 6 years of age. The genetic development of selected motor skills with regard to throwing, catching, kicking, striking, and bouncing was investigated. The purpose of the study was to discover discrete patterns of performance for each of the skills studied and the course of development that these patterns took when viewed in terms of recognized patterns of skillful adult performance. Forty-three girls and boys were used as subjects. Motion pictures of their performance in a partially controlled situation constituted the main body of the data. Through direct observation and cinema-analysis, the element and sequence of the occurrence of growth patterns was defined.

Deach studied growth in accuracy and control in relation to the target by a scatter diagram of hits. Detailed knowledge of the environment was obtained by questions to the parents. Personal data were obtained through school records. The scope was limited by small numbers in each group.

The results showed progression in the development of patterns from simple arm and leg action to highly integrated total body coordinations. For example, in throwing action the progression ranged from the elbow to the shoulder, and in catching, from the arm and body to the fingers. In kicking, progression ranged from no backswing to one originating at the knee, hip, and finally to a full leg swing. Striking evolved from a true throw to a push with one hand, to a hit first overhand, then underhand. Bouncing developed from a single bounce to multiple bounces.

The progression was composed of three basic steps found in all hand-foot patterns from the action of the primary part to opposition and body involvement. The advanced stages approached skillful adult performance.[3]

Guttridge's investigation portrayed the child in his usual activities, under everyday conditions without distraction. The activities chosen were climbing, jumping, sliding, tricycling, hopping, skipping, galloping, and throwing, catching and bouncing balls. Subjects were nine children aged 3 years, 7 months, to 6 years, 8 months, and the study was extended for a period of 1 year. Guttridge reported that girls tend to excel in hopping, skipping, and galloping while boys are superior in jumping and throwing.[4]

Wild utilized cinematography to analyze the throwing patterns of children 2 through 7 years of age. Each subject was asked to perform three overhand throws, which were filmed. Two development trends were found: (1) a gradual shift of movement from a predominantly anterior-posterior plane to a horizontal plane and (2) a transfer from the use of an unchanging base to a shifting base on the same side as the throwing arm followed by weight transfer in a more stable and functional arm-foot relationship. Each change was found to be more effective for the mechanical projection for the acceleration of the ball.[5]

Singer conducted a longitudinal study on the overarm throwing behavior of four young girls, two "poor" and two "good," ages 8 to 11. Filming techniques were used for the analysis of their performances over a 4-year period. The conclusions of Singer indicated that improvement in throwing ability was generally due to (1) a greater range of joint movement and (2) speed, especially in the actions of the torso and medial rotation of the humerus.[6]

Victors undertook a cinematographic analysis of the catching behavior of a selected group of 7- and 9-year-old boys. The purpose of this investigation was to study, by use of cinematography, the catching behavior of twenty selected 7- and 9-year-old boys in an attempt to identify components of catching skill and patterns of motor response that differentiate successful and unsuccessful performance of this skill.

The subjects were selected by successful or an unsuccessful performance on skill measures and subjective ranking. The findings were as follows:

1. The age differences in the frequency of successful performances in catching the ball were not greater than chance.
2. The ball size did not differentiate successful and unsuccessful behavior at these age levels.
3. The components (stance, body alignment, arm positions) were different with each level.
4. The results obtained with simultaneous two-hand closure were significantly different from those obtained when closure was not simultaneous.
5. There was a noticeable development trend evidenced in extraneous movement and hand-arm movement prior to and after contact.[7]

Espenschade and Eckert indicated that cinematographic and electromyographic studies were needed to discover the relationship between physiological maturation and motor behavior patterning, and that it seemed to be an especially fruitful area.[8]

Cooper and Glassow showed figures of a 33-month-old child, studied as he performed various motor patterns. The assessment of these patterns was taken from films of a learning task. "It can be stated with confidence that, even if a child had the opportunity to observe skilled performance, he would not be aware of the details of action." Cooper and Glassow further stated that the elements of skillful performance were present in the throwing performance of a young child.[9]

Hanson conducted a study in which she developed practice sessions designed to influence the development of the overarm throw pattern of 5-year-old children. The guided practice group was taught for a total of fifteen quarter-hour periods. The lessons were designed to give the children practice and instruction in the skill and to increase their basic understanding of the throw. No discussions were held, rather the children were given situations that demanded correct responses in movement. They were placed in a position that demanded opposition to the throw, that is, they were placed in a starting position consistent with the mature pattern when throwing at a wall. Hanson concluded that the throwing patterns of the instructed group did mature more rapidly than the noninstructed group.[10]

Glassow and associates reported a 5-year longitudinal study in the motor performance of elementary school children. The authors felt that the study was unique in that it was longitudinal, enhanced by a yearly filming of the subjects, and concerned with the relationship of strength to the product as made possible by the annual measures of strength and skills.

In their investigations of the coordination of selected fundamental skills, the researchers measured the appearance of the patterns, the achievement of the skills, the coordination of the run, jump, and throw, the effects of practice, and the relationship of strength and skill.

The measures of coordination were accomplished by high speed photography and graphs. Joint action in time depicted the contributions of each segment to the total action, which they felt exemplified the types of measures that would further the understanding of coordination.[11]

Preceding studies indicated that cinematographic procedure had been used recently for the assessment of physical skills and for the documentation of skills or motor patterns in young children. Areas of study included a determination of growth and the development of motor patterns, coordination of gross motor skills, and the relationship of strength development and skill development.

The research included longitudinal and short-term collection of photographic data. Analysis of photographic data varied from subjective observation to analysis of coordinates of time and body segments.

One of the most recent studies on six fundamental motor patterns was conducted by Wickstrom. He selected running, jumping, throwing, catching, kicking, and striking, because he felt that they were the basis of the largest number of skills in the complex stages of movement. Wickstrom's analysis, made from high speed filming of basic patterns, gives an accurate description of the developing stages of the six patterns.[12]

Results of the studies indicated that there was a progression in development of motor patterns in young children and that advanced stages approached skilled adult performance.

CHILD GROWTH AND DEVELOPMENT STUDIES OF MOTOR PATTERNS

Bayley found that the most rapid changes in growth and development take place in the early years, and that gross motor coordinations develop more rapidly than mental functions before two years of age. Bayley also reported higher correlation between mental and motor development at that age than during the following years.[13]

Meyers and associates reported "so little factoral work has been accomplished with young children that most elemental questions one may ask have no answer." They suggested questions for study, such as: "Can differential abilities be demonstrated? If so, at how early an age?" "When, for example, in the normal child's development may one first discern the rudiments of the Guilford structure?"

The purpose of their study was: (1) to hypothesize for domains of the primary abilities well established for adult levels, and by testing, demonstrate them with normal school children of preliterate age (6 years) and (2) to determine whether any factoral differences worthy of note may be seen between normal and retarded children of comparable mental age.

From the results of their research, Meyers and co-workers made these suggestions for obtaining the best results in conducting research with young children: ". . . the preschool child is preliterate: the child cannot read directions or write responses. His cooperation in group examinations is not dependable . . . for usable results an individually administered examination is required."[14]

Fales constructed a rating scale to judge the vigorousness of the play activities of the preschool child. A list of 651 items was formulated from observation and diary records. All activities were play skills. Examples included activities ranging from turning somersaults to hanging by one hand on the jungle gym; sitting and pushing slightly with the feet as well as swinging high using arms and back muscles, rather than pushing with the feet on the swings; running up with heavy object to running down, or rolling down on the incline board; standing and balancing on the middle, to climbing on when the end was high on the seesaw; hanging with both hands to swinging using feet to push on the climbing rope; somersaults, sitting on the top, and balancing on the stomach on the bar; balancing and walking on the balance board; walking on the edge to jumping and moving in and out of the sandbox; throwing small balls with one hand and throwing to somebody or against something, catching the return. This category also included kicking the small ball about; kicking the large ball; running with an object; climbing up and down stairs with alternate feet; skipping with swinging arms; jumping off varying heights; jumping for distance; riding tricycle, kiddie car, and wagon; and various whirls and rolls. The scope of these activities indicates the constant mobility and imagination of the child.[15]

Goodenough and Smart conducted a study on the interrelationships of motor abilities in young children. The introduction contained pertinent comments on the conflicting views in the findings on motor ability. It stated the "possible existence" of a general motor ability not dependent on age, sex, physical size and strength, intelligence, and similar traits. "The question is whether or not motor abilities involving different muscle groups and differing in apparent complexity show any tendency to vary concomitantly in the same individual when the other factors, such as those noted above, are held constant."

Goodenough and Smart felt that the optimum time to study these abilities was in the early years, due to "differential practices" and "unequal motivation from outside sources" that could color the results in later years. This longitudinal study was conducted at the Institute of Child Welfare at the University of Minnesota. The children were tested midway between birthdays at 2½, 3½, 4½, and 5½ years of age. The included items were:

1. Time required to walk a 25-foot line
2. Errors in stepping off the line on the above
3. Finger tapping with the contometer
4. Needle threading test
5. Three hole test
6. Simple reaction time

Findings showed that the children behaved in a uniform fashion and thus could be reliably tested on motor skills. Reliabilities were high ranging from .53 to .94 with most scores in the .80 range.[16]

McCaskill and Wellman made a study of the common motor achievements of the preschool child. The objectives as stated were: (1) to set stages of development for selected motor achievements, (2) the sequence of this development, (3) the interval of the development, and (4) its relation to sex and ascendance scores. The subjects were ninety-eight children from 2 to 6 years in the preschool laboratory at the University of Iowa. The selected activities were:

1. Ascending and descending ladders
2. Ascending and descending steps
3. Hopping, skipping, jumping, and balancing on path and circle
4. Ball throwing, catching, and bouncing

The tests were constructed for simplicity and the ability to be reproduced effectively. All tests had significant reliability. The authors contributed the high reliability of their tests to the fact that the activities were appealing to the children as daily play situations, and similarly enjoyed as "games." It was felt that the performances were normal and therefore representative of the children's ability.

In conclusion, the motor achievements were assigned to age groups. The assignments were made at the point where 50 percent passed and 50 percent failed.

The items were:

Age	Items
36 months	Jumping 28 inches with help
37 months	Walking path, no steps off
37 months	Jumping 18 inches along, feet together
38 months	Hopping on both feet one to three steps
38 months	Ascending small ladder, alternate feet
41 months	Ascending long steps, alternate feet, unsupported
43 months	Throwing large ball, one or both hands
44 months	Throwing small ball, one or both hands
45 months	Walking circle, no steps off
53 months	Descending small ladder, alternate feet, with ease
57 months	Throwing small ball

The boys as a whole tended to be superior in step and ladder tests while the girls were noticeably superior in the hopping and skipping activities.[17]

Jenkins made a comparison of motor achievements of 5-, 6- and 7-year-old children. Three hundred subjects were used, one hundred in each age group divided according to sex. A series of tests chosen as "specimens of the varied types of activities participated in by children" were administered. The tests were:

1. Thirty-five yard dash
2. Beanbag toss for accuracy
3. Baseball throw for distance
4. Soccer kick for distance

5. Baseball throw for accuracy
6. Standing broad jump
7. Running broad jump
8. Jump and reach
9. Fifty-foot hop

They were scored for discrimination rather than pass or fail in order to give the children an opportunity to succeed without undue pressure. In all events the child was encouraged to do his best, and only the best score was recorded. Instructions were the same for all.[18]

Hartman offered a pertinent study on fifty-six children between the ages of 47 and 72 months. It was stimulated by the Cowan and Pratt test, which maintained that the hurdle jump was a definite single indicator of motor coordination for ages 3 to 12 inclusive. A test battery was devised to challenge or agree with that theory. Hartman was also concerned with clarifying the conflicting concepts of motor activity; whether there was a general element of motor ability or there were a number of specific abilities. Four test items were selected based on Jenkins and Carpenter's findings. The items were:

1. The jump and reach
2. Standing broad jump
3. Baseball throw for distance
4. Thirty-five yard dash

Hartman concluded that the other items were as accurate as the hurdle jump for a measurement of motor ability. It was felt that the hurdle jump was not the best single measure of motor proficiency.[19]

Sloan made an adaptation of the Oseretsky Tests of Motor Proficiency and concluded that they could be used as a research tool in the area of child development, with the correction of weaknesses. Sloan adapted thirty-six of the original eighty-five items, and arranged them according to the degree of difficulty, ascertained by the percentage passing. The test items were geared more to the fine motor coordinations than the gross motor skills. Several tests were omitted because of possible injury to the child. The gross motor tests included were:

1. Walking backwards
2. Crouching on tiptoes
3. Standing on one foot
4. Jumping over a rope
5. Standing heel to toe
6. Catching a ball

7. Jumping in the air, making an about face, landing on tiptoes and holding for three seconds
8. Throwing a ball (shot put fashion)
9. Balancing on tiptoes
10. Jumping and touching heels
11. Standing on one foot with eyes closed
12. Jumping and clapping
13. Balancing on tiptoes

Sloan felt that the test was valid in containing a comprehensive area of motor abilities, discrimination of ages, and showing positive correlations with other motor ability tests, although low.

The entire battery was made up of a wide range of items in time motor coordinations, gross motor activities, unilateral and bilateral attempts.[20]

Interest in child growth and development in the 1930s is evidenced by the number of studies reviewed. The focus was mainly a catalogue-type documentation of the abilities of children. The development of physical skill was recorded through observations and by structured, self-testing situations.

Testing was conducted for the construction of valid and reliable motor ability tests for preschool age children.

From these studies, it was found that young children possessed a wide range of physical abilities, and that they could be reliably tested on these abilities.

STUDIES WITH IMPLICATIONS FOR YOUNG CHILDREN

Singer discussed the impact of early experience that has been explained through the recently popularized "stage" approach. At present, many psychologists believe that children do not go through the same experiences according to their age, but rather according to critical periods or stages.[21]

Oxendine supports this theory when he states that: "Motor skills are not developed until the child's neuromuscular system is sufficiently ready. When the required maturation level has been reached the responses (grasping, walking, talking, etc.) will normally be made . . ." The child can be trained more easily and quickly if he has reached a full state of physiological readiness for the specific activity.

He further states that he feels that the role of the teacher and the parent in promoting motor skill learning would be to determine the time at

Fig. 2-2

which children are ready to learn specific motor patterns and then arrange a learning environment that would be most effective for their development.[22]

Research in maturation has generally been designed to determine: (1) at what age certain types of skills can be learned most effectively and (2) if special training can speed the learning of certain skills.

According to Piaget's stages of intellectual development, by 2 years of age the child has acquired sensorimotor control, and that by the 2- to 4-year old stage the child is capable of extracting concepts from experiences. This system might be applicable to education by telling us something about the most favorable conditions for learning, and hence the way we should go about teaching.[23]

Piaget's "Penser, c'est operer"[24] indicates that the learner must be led to perform real actions on the materials to form a learning base, actions that are as concrete and direct as the materials can be made to be. As the actions are repeated and varied, they begin to intercoordinate with each other and also to become schematic and internalized. The next step then is to differentiate the specific physical actions to or engendering a given phenomenon and then having the student practice them.[25]

Landers conducted a study on the correlation of anxiety and performance in young children as influenced by acquiescence. The finding indicated that there was no significant effect of acquiescence on performance.[26]

Martens conducted a study on the effects of social reinforcement on children's motor performance and found that no significant effects were obtained. The results showed that preschool boys were significantly superior to preschool girls on the throwing motor task that was used with the twenty-five boys and twenty-five girls tested.[27]

Jeanrenaud and Linford conducted a study of twenty preschool children between the ages of 3 and 5 years old in relation to their approach behavior to a piece of novel play apparatus. Findings indicated that avoidance behavior decreases upon repeated exposure to a novel situation.[28]

Godfrey and Kephart stated that the learning situation for the preschool child is hierarchic in form. Further, certain skills require previous learning of basics, and complex skills are not presented until the child has acquired a readiness for them.[29]

Godfrey and Kephart consider readiness to be the result of maturation and learning. They report that motor learning makes up a large portion of the development of readiness skills in young children. "The motor activities of the child, therefore, become important not only for their own sake, but for the contribution which they must make to more complex activities which he will be required to perform later."[29]

Clifton and Smith at Purdue are conducting longitudinal studies on the developmental stages of motor skills in young children.[30]

Researchers were principally concerned with the contributions that motor skills could make to enhance the learning process and to the development of readiness and maturation during preschool years.

REFERENCES

1. Sinclair, Caroline: Movement and movement patterns of childhood, Richmond, Va., 1971, State Department of Education, Division of Educational Research and Statistics, p. 22.
2. Halverson, Lolas E.: Development of motor patterns in young children, Quest **6:**44-53, 1969.
3. Deach, Dorothy F.: Genetic development of motor skills in children two through six years of age, Microfilm Abstracts **11:**278-280.
4. Guttridge, Mary V.: A study of motor achievements of young children, Archives of Psychology **244:**1-178, 1939.
5. Wild, Monica R.: The behavior pattern of throwing and some observations concerning its course of development in children, Ph.D. dissertation, University of Wisconsin, 1961.
6. Singer, Francine: Comparison of the development of the overarm throwing patterns of good and poor performers (girls), Master's thesis, University of Wisconsin, 1961.
7. Victors: Evelyn E.: A cinematographical analysis of catching behavior of a selected group of seven and nine year old boys, Dissertation Abstracts **22:**1903-1904, 1961.
8. Espenschade, Anna, and Eckert, Helen M.: Motor development, Columbus, Ohio, 1967, Charles E. Merrill Publishing Co., p. 136.
9. Cooper, John M., and Glassow, Ruth B.: Kinesiology, ed. 1, St. Louis, 1963, The C. V. Mosby Co., p. 57-61.
10. Hanson, Sue K.: A comparison of the overhand throw performance of instructed and non-instructed kindergarten boys and girls, Master's thesis, University of Wisconsin, 1961.
11. Glassow, Ruth B., et al.: Improvement of motor development and physical fitness in elementary school children, unpublished material, Cooperative Research Project No. 696, USOE Research Grant and University of Wisconsin Research Foundation, 1969.
12. Wickstrom, Ralph L.: Fundamental motor patterns, Philadelphia, 1970, Lea & Febiger.
13. Bayley, Nancy: The development of motor abilities during the first two years, Society for Research in Child Development Monographs, No. 1, 1936, pp. 1-26.
14. Meyers, Carl E., et al.: Primary abilities at mental age six, Society for Research in Child Development Monographs, XXVII, 1962, p. 3.
15. Fales, Evaline: A rating scale of the vigorousness of play activities of preschool children, Child Development **8:**15-144, 1937.
16. Goodenough, Florence L., and Smart, Russel C.: Inter-relationships of motor abilities in young children, Child Development **6:**141-153, 1935.
17. McCaskill, Carra Lou, and Wellman, Beth L.: A study of common motor achievements at the preschool ages, Child Development **9:**141-150, 1938.
18. Jenkins, Lulu M.: A comparative study of motor achievements of children at five, six, and seven years of age, Contributions to Education, No. 114, New York, 1930, Teachers College, Columbia University.
19. Hartman, Doris M.: The hurdle jump as a measure of motor proficiency, Child Development **14:**201-211, 1943.

20. Sloan, William: The Lincoln-Oseretsky motor development scale, Genetic Society Monographs **52:**183-252, 1955.
21. Singer, Robert N.: Motor learning and human performance, New York, 1968, The Macmillan Co., p. 72.
22. Oxendine, Joseph B.: Psychology of motor learning, New York, 1968, Appleton-Century-Crofts, pp. 139-140.
23. Flavell, John H.: The developmental psychology of Jean Piaget, New York, 1963, Van Nostrand Reinhold Co., pp. 365-366.
24. Aebli, H.: Didactique psychologique: application a la didactique de la psychologie de Jean Piaget, Neuchatel, Switzerland, 1951, Delachaux & Niestle, p. 73.
25. Flavell: Psychology of Piaget, p. 368.
26. Landers, Daniel M.: Acquiescence and the motor performance of high anxious subjects, unpublished, Motor Performance and Play Research Laboratory, University of Illinois, 1969-1970.
27. Martens, Rainer: Social reinforcement effects on preschool children's motor performance, unpublished, Children's Research Center, University of Illinois, 1969-1970.
28. Jeanrenaud, Claudine Y., and Linford, Anthony G.: Approach-avoidance behavior of young childen in a novel play environment, U. S. Public Health Service Research Grant No. NB-07346, and State of Illinois Department of Mental Health, 1969.
29. Godfrey, Barbara B., and Kephart, Newell C.: Movement patterns and motor education, New York, 1969, Appleton-Century-Crofts.
30. Clifton, Margarite, and Smith, Hope (Research in progress, Purdue University, Indiana.)

chapter 3

Motor pattern development in children

INTRODUCTION

What is in store for the child of the future? Toffler thinks that schools of tomorrow should see that the child is versatile and "grounded in certain common skills needed for human communication and social integration."[2] This concept suggests a shift to the humanistic curriculum rather than the subject curriculum.

Many theories for intervention in early childhood development have been proposed ranging from compulsory day care centers to "ecological intervention,"[3] which involves cultural development enhancement systems. States have proposed new early childhood education systems, and parent–child care centers have been funded throughout the country. Focus on the education of the young child is the major contemporary social action.

There seems to be no question that young children should be placed in learning environments. The premise of this book is, therefore, that the environments include movement as one of the basic learning tools when working with young children ages 2 through 6 (Fig. 3-1).

BASIC MOTOR PATTERN DEVELOPMENT

It is my belief that very young children do not learn by being forced to adhere to adult patterns of complex skills for games, but rather de-

25

Fig. 3-1. (Courtesy Educational Facilities Laboratories, New York. Photograph by Ron Partridge.)

Fig. 3-2

velop the basic patterns naturally through stimulations, challenges, and extrinsic motivations by parents and peers. This idea is reinforced by research in which children between the ages of 2 to 6 years showed observable improvement in basic motor patterns of jumping, kicking, striking, and throwing after repeated performance with encouragement but no instruction.[4] (Fig. 3-2.)

Note the observable improvement of the pattern even though no instruction was given. The child was only encouraged to "throw harder," for example.

In the study, a comparison was made between the child's motor pattern and the same pattern of a skilled performer (Fig. 3-3).

Analysis of the two patterns indicates that the performance of the basic pattern is identical. Obviously, the results of the action would be different, since strength and speed and other factors are involved in the mature pattern, but the basic pattern with joint angles and preparatory action and follow-through phases are the same.

It seems that the formative stages of the basic patterns occur between the ages of 18 months and 60 months. After that time, basic pattern development is relatively stable (Fig. 3-4).

Following this thought, incorrectly formed patterns would need remedial correction after 5 years of age. For example, many females and some males never develop a mature throwing pattern, but continue to throw inefficiently in adult life. This example would indicate that the pattern never developed during the formative stage, probably because of the pursuit of passive rather than active activities. It appears that children who are active in a variety of movement activities develop better motor skills naturally.

ANALYSIS OF BASIC PATTERNS

Teachers of movement in early childhood should be able to recognize correctly executed motor patterns. A motor pattern is a series of movements put together to achieve a purpose. Each pattern has three phases: preparatory, action, and follow-through. Figs. 3-5 to 3-7 illustrate the breakdown of the three phases of the throwing pattern whose objective or purpose is to throw or project an object.

LEARNING MODULE
Instructional module for learning about motor skills

The objective of this instructional module is to provide basic observational and analysis competencies involving basic motor skills in early child-

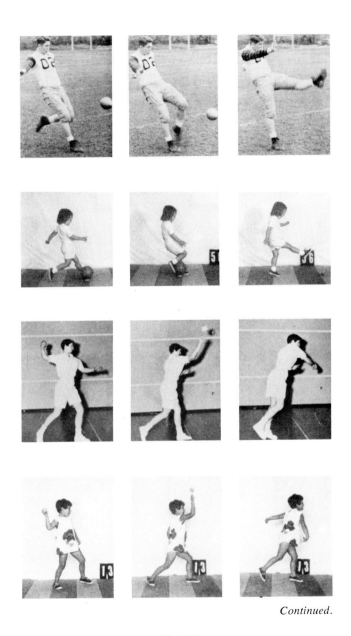

Continued.

Fig. 3-3

Fig. 3-3, cont'd

Fig. 3-4

hood. At the conclusion of this module, you will be able to know fundamental concepts, exhibit a variety of desirable observation and analysis
skills, and apply the above in a practical movement education situation.
Once you have met the minimum proficiency established for the above, you
will apply these skills in a field experience that will serve as the postassess-
ment for this instructional module.

Preassessment

Before beginning this module, you should determine at what point you
will enter the instructional sequence of this module. On the next pages
you will find a series of questions. Provide written responses in as many
areas as possible and score yourself according to the instructions provided. This is not a test. The purpose is solely that of determining knowledge you may have already acquired, thereby saving you a needless repetition of study. Below you will find a series of statements. Without looking
at any instructional materials, provide the appropriate term or concept.

Preassessment instrument

    1. Define the following four terms:
        a. Form discrimination   c. Laterality
        b. Kinesthetic   d. Spatial localization

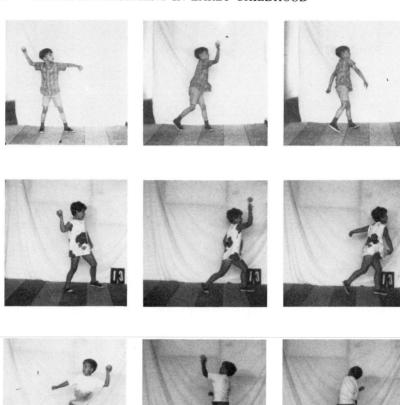

Fig. 3-5

2. List the five major neuromuscular maturation stages in children from 1 to 5 years of age.
3. Define four elements of movement.
4. Describe the three elements in a movement pattern.
5. Describe the four perceptual motor body movement factors.

With the exercise you just completed and for all exercises and criterion tests included in this module, the minimum proficiency level has been established as 95 percent. In order to achieve this percentage, you had to have a minimum of nineteen correct responses. If you accomplished this goal, you do not need to study the rest of the module. If you did not have nineteen correct responses, continue through this module.

Teachers "know" most of what they learn about children by observing

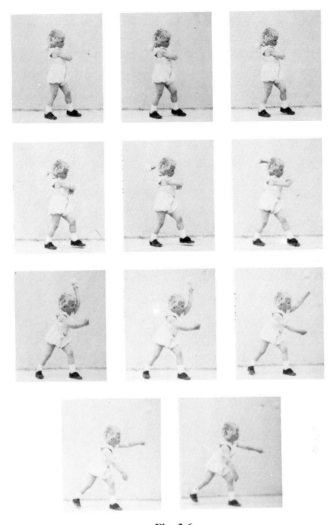

Fig. 3-6

them. When selected, specific concepts are apparent, teachers know what they are looking for, and observations can be focused on evidence relating to such concepts.

To aid in this need for accurate observations, a checklist instrument has been designed that you should be able to apply to observations of young children. One thing that is important for you to realize is that this, or any other checklist, is limited to the evaluation of visible and readily ascertained behaviors. Therefore, a variety of instruments are available and you may eventually want to design your own to meet highly specific needs.

Fig. 3-7

Below are samples of the checklist instruments. Once you have filled in the profile sheet, match your rating scales with another student.

CHECKLIST INSTRUMENT

NAME OF CHILD_____AGE_____

DATE_____

EXAMINER_____SEX_____

	Yes	*No*	*Comments*
1. Able to maintain balance without falling (on a plank)			
2. Able to walk and run with smooth bodily movements			
3. Able to jump up and down adequately			
4. Able to climb and hang with confidence			
5. Able to catch a ball accurately			
6. Able to reach and grasp adequately			

If an accurate profile record is to be constructed for an individual, you must be able to watch a child move and to correctly record the movements. The observation-record method will enhance your ability to analyze movement behavior.

The purpose of this objective is to make it possible for you to construct a profile sheet that records the observation of stipulated movements performed by the preschool-age child. (See p. 36.)

As with previous exercises, a perfect match would be extremely difficult as you review your observations with one of your colleagues. After discussing and resolving the differences, if any, begin your study of the next objective.

The elements of movement

The student should be able to recognize movement elements in order to analyze the movement behavior of young children, and then to constructively assist the children in solving their movement problems after the analysis. Upon completing the preceding objectives, you should have the ability to define four elements of movement: time, weight, space, and force. In addition you should have ability to recognize the movement elements in observing the action patterns of children and be able to apply these behaviors in an instructional situation with young children.

On p. 37 is a chart that supplies definitions of the four selected movements that includes the ways in which these movements are used. Using a similar chart, select a child and record the gross motor skills of the child. Upon completion check your work with the sample chart.

Pretest yourself by answering the following questions:

1. Describe the four movement elements.
2. Give an example of a gross motor skill and cite the use of each element in a skilled pattern.

The elements in a movement pattern

During observations of perceptual motor skills of children you should be aware of the complete pattern of movement. This will enable you to formulate a movement analysis repertoire to be used in perceptual motor instruction.

Upon the conclusion of your work in this area you will be able to define three elements of the movement patttern and describe the individual elements in the performance of the movement pattern. In order

CHECKLIST INSTRUMENT

MOVEMENT SKILLS	TIMES OBSERVED	VARIETY OBSERVED
Balancing	Involved in all skills	Dynamic balance
Bouncing	xxxxx xx	1. At different levels
		2. One hand
		3. Two hands
		4. Alternate hands
		5. While jumping rope
		6. While walking ladder
		7. Around self
Carrying	All ball skills	1. Carrying ball
		2. Carrying loop
Catching	xx	1. From wall
		2. On upward throws
Climbing		
Crawling	xx	1. To retrieve flag
		2. With ball bounce
Forward roll		
Galloping		
Hanging		
Hitting	x	Baseball swing from tee
Hopping		
Kicking	x	Dribble
Jumping	xx	Over rope with alternate feet
Leaping	x	To retrieve flag
Pulling		
Pushing		
Running	xxxx	1. Through ladder
		2. Around obstacle
		3. After partner
		4. Between tracks
Skipping	x	Around obstacle
Sliding	xxx	1. With ball
		2. Around obstacles
		3. In flag game
Throwing	xxxxx	1. Overhand one hand at target
		2. Two hand upward
		3. One hand against wall
		4. Two hand underhand at target
		5. One hand underhand at target
Walking	xx	1. Through ladder
		2. Between tracks

Checklist

	MOVEMENT USED	HOW ELEMENT USED
Time		
Time sequence of the movement	1. Somersault 2. Jumping over object 3. Handstand	1. Fast 2. Quick 3. Sustained
Weight		
Part or parts of the body support-ing the weight	1. Somersault 2. Jumping over object 3. Handstand	1. Hands, back, feet 2. Feet 3. Hands
Space		
Directions or levels of movement	1. Somersault 2. Jumping over object 3. Handstand	1. Forward; on mat level 2. Forward; elevated level 3. Stationary; floor level
Force		
Quality of muscular force used	1. Somersault 2. Jumping over object 3. Handstand	1. Not controlled, tension less 2. Sufficient force applied to get over object 3. Controlled tension

to gain a working knowledge of the phases of the movement pattern, review the phases of a movement pattern and Fig. 3-3.

On p. 38 is a checklist used for charting specific motor skills. Construct a similar checklist with the activities kick, throw, and jump and analyze the patterns for one child in each of three action phases.

If your analysis is similar to the sample checklist, you are ready for the self-assessment check below. If there were marked differences, make arrangements to study them with one of your colleagues before taking the self-assessment check.

Self-assessment check for previous objective

1. Distinguish a complete pattern from an incomplete pattern.
2. Isolate the three phases of a complete pattern.
3. Isolate the beginning point of the preparatory phase, the action phase, and the follow-through phase.
4. Correct an incomplete pattern.

Factors that affect movement responses

When observing children, it is critical for you to have a knowledge of basic movement factors that are most related to motor skills. The purpose of the objective is to provide you with the ability to define and describe

Checklist

	1ST KICK	2ND THROW	3RD JUMP
Preparatory phase	1. Trunk extended	1. Trunk rotated clockwise	1. Trunk flexed
	2. Knee flexed	2. Wrist extended	2. Knees flexed
	3. Ankle flexed	3. Elbow flexed	3. Ankles flexed
	4. Body leaned backward	4. Shoulder extended	4. Arms extended
	5. Arms used in opposition	5. Arms and legs placed in opposition	5. Shoulders extended
		6. Weight on rear foot	6. Head forward
Action phase	1. Trunk starts flexing	1. Trunk rotated counter clockwise	1. Trunk extended
	2. Knee extended	2. Elbows flexed	2. Knees extended
	3. Ankle locked	3. Wrist flexed	3. Ankles extended
	4. Body leaned back	4. Shoulder flexed	4. Arms extended upward
	5. Arms used in opposition	5. Arms and legs used in opposition	5. Shoulders flexed
		6. Weight transfering	6. Head backward
Follow-through phase	1. Trunk hyperflexed	1. Trunk rotated counter clockwise	1. Trunk flexed
	2. Knee fully extended	2. Wrist flexed	2. Knees flexed
	3. Ankle fully extended	3. Elbow extended	3. Ankles flexed
	4. Body leaned backward	4. Shoulder flexed	4. Arms forward
	5. Arms in opposition for balance	5. Arms and legs are in position	5. Shoulders flexed
		6. Weight on forward foot	6. Head forward

the four movement factors of body awareness, spatial awareness, quality or force, and relationships. In addition, you will be able to recognize examples of movement that exemplify these factors.

On p. 40 is a checklist used to describe factors that affect movement. Construct a similar checklist, and when you have completed your work compare it with the sample.

Fig. 3-8

Checklist

Give three examples of a movement or skill to enhance factors 1, 2, 3, and 4.

1. *Body awareness* Awareness of body parts, and front, side, and back	1. Lying on back 2. Throwing with right hand 3. Rolling ball with foot
2. *Spatial awareness* Awareness of body in relation to objects or persons and directions	1. Jumping over object 2. Throwing at a target 3. Walking through a ladder
3. *Quality of force* Awareness of movements for hard, soft, fast, and slow efforts	1. Running quickly 2. Twisting slowly 3. Hopping softly
4. *Relationships* Awareness of body in dynamic balance and moving situations	1. Running among moving objects 2. Striking a thrown ball 3. Working with partner and objects

Self-assessment check

Answer the following statements:
1. Define each movement factor.
2. Cite a movement that would illustrate each of the factors above.

Key for self-assessment

1. Define each movement factor:
   Body awareness knowledge of the whole body and its parts
   Spatial awareness knowledge of the body in relation to space
   Force knowledge of the strength of the movement
   Relationship knowledge of the moving body in relation to moving objects
2. Cite a movement that would illustrate each of the preceding factors:
   Lifting right or left hand
   Running to the right or left
   Moving fast or slow
   Catching a thrown ball

Terminal objective 4

This is the terminal objective of the module. In this objective you will exhibit the desired teacher-learning behaviors that have been learned in previous objectives while working with young children in a laboratory experience.

Applying these competencies will give you an opportunity to see if the teacher behaviors that were learned will be successful in helping you to enhance the learning of motor skills by young children.

Activity I. Select one objective and apply it to working with a group of young children.

Activity II. Make your own evaluation instrument and apply it to the analysis of the motor skills of several young children.

Activity III. Plan and conduct a lesson for young children using basic motor skills.

Since we know that the child can develop through the motor levels of reflex movements and basic patterns by age 5, it seems plausible to include learning activities in the perceptual-motor and skill development as a sequential movement curriculum for the young child. It is possible that many children will be able to participate in a degree of movements. Through the movement-education approach, each child will be challenged at his own rate and readiness and improve according to each one's ability. The next chapter will explain the program design for learning through movement activities.

REFERENCES

1. Mead, Margaret: Culture and commitment: a study of the generation gap, Garden City, N. Y., 1970, Doubleday and Co., Inc., p. 72.
2. Toffler, Alvin.: Future shock, New York 1970, Random House, Inc., p. 366.
3. Bronfenbrenner, Urie: Is early intervention effective? presentation to National Association for Education of Young Children, Atlanta, November, 1972.
4. Flinchum, Betty M.: Selected motor patterns of preschool age children, Ph.D. dissertation, Louisiana State University, 1971.
5. Broer, Marion: Efficiency of human movement, ed. 3, Philadelphia, 1960, W. B. Saunders Co., p. 18.
6. Cooper, John M., and Glassow, Ruth B.: Kinesiology, St. Louis, 1963, The C. V. Mosby Co., pp. 132-133, 148.

chapter 4

Understanding the psychomotor domain

The teacher of the young child should have a sound knowledge of the psychomotor domain in order to plan movement activities in that domain. It can always be used as a resource and reference for sequence and continuum.

To help those working with young children understand the elements of movement to be used, the stages of development through movement and the learning stages have been provided. Table 2 shows the motor classification and the learning stages in the motor domain.

There are many classifications of the psychomotor domain available for reference in curriculum development for young children, of which Corbin[1] and Simpson[2] would be examples. However, the material in this book has been based on the works of Anita J. Harrow.[3]

THE PSYCHOMOTOR DOMAIN

Following the development of the basic fundamental movements, which are a basis for complex movement skills, the child is ready for perceptual-motor and purposeful movements. (Fig. 4-1.)

Table 1 outlines the projected activities for early childhood based on Harrow's taxonomy for the motor domain.[3]

Table 1. Taxonomy for the psychomotor domain: classification levels and subcategories[3]

TAXONOMY CONTINUUM	LEVELS	DEFINITIONS	BEHAVIORAL ACTIVITY
1.10 Segmental 1.20 Interseg- mental 1.30 Supraseg- mental	1.00 Reflex movements	Actions elicited without conscious voli- tion in response to some stimuli	Flexion, extension, stretch, postural adjustments
2.10 Locomotor 2.20 Nonloco- motor 2.30 Manipulative	2.00 Basic fundamen- tal movements	Required: level 1.00 Inherent movement patterns that are formed from a combining of reflex movements, and are the basis for complex skilled movement	2.10 Walking, running, jumping, sliding, hopping, rolling, climbing 2.20 Pushing, pulling, swaying, swinging, stop- ping, stretching, bending, twisting 2.30 Handling, manipulating, gripping, grasping finger movements
3.10 Kinesthetic discrimi- nation 3.20 Visual dis- crimination 3.30 Auditory discrimina- tion 3.40 Tactile dis- crimination 3.50 Coordinated abilities	3.00 Perceptual abilities	Required: level 1.00 to 2.00 Interpretation of stimuli from various modalities providing data for the learner to make adjustments to his environment	The outcomes of perceptual abilities are observable in all purposeful movement. Examples: Auditory—following verbal instructions Visual—dodging a moving ball Kinesthetic—making bodily adjustments in a hand-stand to maintain balance Tactile—determining texture through touch Coordinated—jump rope, punting, catching

4.00 Physical abilities	Functional characteristics of organic vigor that are essential to the development of highly skilled movement
4.10 Endurance	All activities that require strenuous effort for long periods of time. Examples: distance running, distance swimming
4.20 Strength	All activities that require muscular exertion. Examples: weight lifting, wrestling
4.30 Flexibility	All activities that require wide range of motion at hip joints. Examples: touching toes, back bend, ballet exercises
4.40 Agility	All activities that require quick precise movements. Examples: shuttle run, typing, dodgeball
5.00 Skilled movements	A degree of efficiency when performing complex movement tasks that are based upon inherent movement patterns
5.10 Simple adaptive skill	All skilled activities that build upon the inherent locomotor and manipulative movement patterns of classification level 2.00
5.20 Compound adaptive skill	
5.30 Complex adaptive skill	These activities are obvious in sports, recreation, dance, and fine arts areas
6.00 Nondiscursive communication	Communication through bodily movement ranging from facial expressions through sophisticated choreographies
6.10 Expressive movement	Body postures, gestures, facial expressions, all efficiently executed skilled dance movements and choreographies
6.20 Interpretive movement	

Fig. 4-1

LEARNING LEVELS

I. Imitation

At this stage, the learner, exposed to an observable action, begins to make covert imitation of that action. Imitation begins with an inner rehearsal of the muscular system, which is guided by an inner push or an impulse to imitate action. Such covert behavior appears to be the starting point in the growth of psychomotor skill. This is then followed by overt performance of an act and capacity to repeat it. The performance, however, lacks neuromuscular coordination or control, and hence is generally in a crude and imperfect form, especially in the very young child. A large percentage of the preschool child's learning takes place at this level.

II. Manipulation

At this stage the learner is capable of performing an act according to instruction rather than just on the basis of observation. Naturally, the development of skill is enhanced by repeated performance of the selected action. Problem solving can occur here.

III. Conceptualization

At this stage the learner achieves at a higher level of refinement in reproducing a given act. Here, accuracy, proportion, and exactness in performance become significant. The next higher subcategory in this class of behaviors makes the learner independent of his original source that guided his action. Accuracy, balance, and other precision skills can be achieved by the preschool child at this level.

IV. Discrimination

At this stage the learner achieves a coordination of a series of acts by establishing appropriate sequence and accomplishing integration or internal consistency among different acts. Rhythmic and complex eye-hand coordination skills begin to appear.

V. Naturalization

At this stage, the learner attains performance at its highest level of proficiency and the act is performed with the least expenditure of psychic energy. The act is routinized to such an extent that it results in automatic and spontaneous response. Walking would be one motor act that has been developed by preschool-age children to the naturalization level. Other

Table 2. Learning levels and psychomotor domain[2]

MOTOR CLASSIFICATION[3]	IMITATION	MANIPU-LATION	CONCEPTUAL-IZATION	DISCRIMI-NATION	NATURAL-IZATION
Reflex movements					
Basic movements	x	x			x
Perceptual activities	x	x			x
Physical abilities				x	x
Skilled movements	x		x	x	x
Nondiscursive movements			x	x	x

basic skills may have been developed, depending on the amount of exposure and challenge to the young child.

Table 2 shows a suggested learning classification for motor development, based on the psychomotor domain.

THE MOTOR TAXONOMY APPLIED TO YOUNG CHILDREN (2 to 6)

The psychomotor taxonomy in this chapter will refer to voluntary movement, and it will be applied to the expected developmental levels of the very young child of 2 to 6 years of age.

Reflex movements

Reflex actions are involuntary, and therefore serve as a fundamental element in motor development. The teacher of the young child should be aware of the reflex movements to understand the continuum of motor development. Neuromuscular maturation and postural development are basic stages that precede the motor act of walking and other other forms of fundamental movement. This book will concern the next five levels of the motor domain. For further reading, Delacato, Cratty, and McGraw offer readings on the knowledge of neuromuscular development during the first years of life.

Basic movements

The preschool age child is developing the basic movements upon which he depends to further develop motor skills. It is the most critical time, at this age, for basic motor patterns to be developed correctly. It is interesting to note that most children develop the movements *on their own*. A natural motor pattern evolves as the child continually explores, or "practices" the pattern. This is the time when preschool educators should be concentrating on the basic motor patterns. A well-planned environment at home, at a children's learning center, or in a kindergarten could ensure the mastery of basic motor patterns at this optimum stage.

It is probable that if this optimum developmental level passes without mastery, remedial learning will have to be planned, and as a result, there can be no guarantee that the child's motor behavior will be as complete or as efficient in later life.

Perceptual-motor movement (Fig. 4-2)

The next level of motor development builds on the learning of the previous stages, and adds another dimension, perception, prior to motor response. In this motor area, the child obtains sensory input, and interprets it before responding with a movement. It seems reasonable to assume that this is a very important area to develop in the young child since cognitive excellence is important to symbolic and conceptual learning, a highly valued skill in the pursuit of academic achievement. Since this has been considered an important area for the motor development of preschool age children, Chapter 5 will be devoted to perceptual-motor learning in more detail.

Physical abilities

Physical abilities are the movements that enable complex skilled movement to be performed. They are the elements that determine "how well" a child performs or that differentiate between the performances of children. A very young child has limitations in this motor development area if his movements have been restricted. Planning the opportunity for the development of this area is essential if the child is to be ready to learn highly skilled movements.

Preschool children do possess physical abilities for adequate performance and these motor abilities can be measured as shown by studies.[4] Skilled movements are dependent on the physical abilities for efficiency and function.

Fig. 4-2

Skilled movements

A skilled movement requires having the ability to perform a complex action or movement pattern with high degree of proficiency. It usually combines several movement elements, and incorporates all of the motor development factors previously learned.

Sports and dance skills are classified in this level of motor development. Preschool-age children may be able to achieve this level; an example is, the publicized preschool-age swimmers. A preschool-age child can be expected to "master" a skill, but may do so at the expense of gaining a high level of basic motor development in the first four levels of the motor domain, and may therefore be deprived of a total motor behavior readiness for all complex skills when needed.

Creative movements

Communication through movement makes up this motor development category. Expressive and interpretative motor development occurs in this area. In planning creative movements for preschool-age children, environmental stimulants such as design, art, and music are good motivators and can be used to obtain good results with young children.

Language arts are useful motivators for the development of creative motor responses. This is an important area for young children and should be accented in the curriculum.

REFERENCES

1. Corbin, Charles B.: Motor development, Dubuque, Iowa, 1973, William C. Brown Company, Publishers.
2. Simpson, Elizabeth Jane: The classification of educational objectives: psychomotor domain, Research Project No. OE 5-85-104, Urbana, 1966, University of Illinois Press.
3. Harrow, Anita J.: A taxonomy of the psychomotor domain, New York, 1973, David McKay Co., Inc.
4. Engstrom, G., editor: The significance of the young child's motor development, Washington, D. C., 1971, AAHPER and NAEYC.

chapter 5

Movement and dance activities

This chapter deals with activities designed for motor development. The activities are arranged according to taxonomy and according to purpose. The purpose is both for motor skill development and for growth in all facets. As the child performs the gross motor activities, a development of the total child is taking place. The self-concept is greatly enhanced, for example, upon repeated successes in moving along with increased knowledge of the body parts and what the body can do. Reflex activities will be limited in the suggested activities because the child of two will have developed beyond the optimum level for enrichment and refinement of those primary motor acts.

Perhaps the optimum level for the refinement of skills through the third level of the taxonomy should occur during 1½ to 5 years of age. Those activities will be cited here in the form in which they could be presented. In presenting the activities, the teacher should utilize the materials in the chapters on management and teaching strategies in order to present a total learning environment. Only the *content* of the movement sessions will be included here. Prior to any program planning for fundamental movements, an assessment should be made of the abilities of the children. Many achievement levels will have been attained by the children at each age and level of development. To facilitate assessment of their motor skill, a motor ability test battery and a perceptual-motor test has been included in the Appendix. In addition, Cratty has provided several tests in his book, *Perceptual Motor*

Efficiency in Children.[1] There are other books that will require very little research to discover and will enable you to choose the one which best fits the situation.

REFLEX MOVEMENTS

Reflex movements are those that are made without conscious thought in response to a stimuli. Movement tasks that build on basic development of postural, segmental, and prehensile reflexes:

Standing tall, on one foot
Walking on a line, different curves and shapes
Walking on a beam, different surfaces
Stretching at levels, widths with different base of support
Twisting, curling on small base of support
Carrying objects on head
Ducking and dodging fleece balls and balloons
Running in and out of moving objects
Hanging on rungs of different sizes

Only a few suggestions for reflex activities have been given to show that they are activities that will be duplicated in the basic or fundamental movement training. There are two basic types of reflexes that occur in the movements of the children; segmental and intersegmental: they precede the basic movements of walking, running, and so forth.

BASIC MOVEMENTS

These basic movements can occur with the neuromuscular maturation of the child and are those motor patterns that form the basis for skilled movements. They are in three categories: locomotor, nonlocomotor, and manipulative.

Locomotor: crawling, sliding, walking, running, jumping, hopping, rolling, climbing.

Nonlocomotor: pushing, pulling, stretching, curling, swinging, bending, twisting.

Manipulative: prehension and dexterity and coordination movements (Fig. 5-1).

Movement tasks that enhance the development and refinement of basic movements:

Body image activities (improve self-concept)

Hide parts of the body: nose, toes, knees, back, and so forth
Lie on back, front, side

Fig. 5-1

Support weight on different parts of the body: feet, shoulders
Move arms, legs, head, feet, and hands to rhythms
Place objects on different parts of the body
Lead with different parts of the body
Draw parts of the body on brown paper
Trace the outline of partner on brown paper
Move body parts in specific directions
Imitate the movement of a specific part of the body
Explore the different ways a body part can move
Have child touch different body parts with his eyes closed
Have children propel objects with different parts of the body
Play games such as looby-lou, Simon says, hokey pokey
Have child respond to mirror images of partner (move the part the
    partner moves)
Have child watch in mirror movement of different parts (use
    rhythms, music, percussion)

COORDINATION ACTIVITIES

To be coordinated a child must be able to move skillfully and freely, so that he will be free to interpret information coming from surroundings. Lack of coordination can be caused by a lack of movement during infancy and early childhood. Every effort should be made to encourage a wide variety of coordinated movement experiences.

Walking

Exploration of many ways of walking, running, jumping:
Walk sidewise (shuffle step)
Walk sidewise (crossover step)
Walk toes out, heels together
Do other ways of walking
Run with hands over head
Run with hands on hip
Run with hands locked behind you
Run on toes
Two feet up and down
One foot, up and down
Jump forward
Jump backward
Jump sidewise, left and right
Jump and turn one fourth, one half, and all the way around

Pushing and pulling

Tug of war—use short rope, one against one
Snake—lie on back, arms together over head, bend body at hips and waistline to right and left
Fish—swim on floor (on stomach)
Bear crawl—right arm and right leg, left arm and left leg

Eye-hand coordination

Balloon batting—have child attempt to keep inflated balloon in air by batting it with open hands. Two or more children may play together.
Beanbag toss—have children toss beanbag in bucket or container with a similar size opening.
Pegs and pegboard—hand pegs to child, one at a time, being sure that he looks at it when he grasps it, then direct him to place the peg in the specific hole.

Plastic ball hit—hang a plastic ball from string, direct child to keep ball moving by batting it with palm, touching it with one finger as it swings toward child. Have child try to put finger in a hole of swinging perforated plastic ball.

Cup-o-ball—have child try to get the ball in the cup.

BALANCE ACTIVITIES

Balance is the ability of the child to sustain control of the body when using both sides simultaneously, individually, or alternately. If a child has good balance, his body acts in an integrated manner, allowing him to develop the ability to sit and to lengthen his attention span.

Stair climbing—child walks raising the knees very high.

Elephant walk—have child bend forward at the waist, allowing the arms to hang limp, clasp hands. Encourage creative interpretation.

Knee walk—children walk on knees, hands in air. Ask for variations.

Duck walk—child places hands behind back for a tail and walks forward, or any reasonable variation.

Bunny hop—have child hop forward on both feet.

Crab walk—have child sit on the floor, place hands palms down behind back. Walk on hands and feet in a backward direction. Ask for variations.

Have child stand on balanced board and tip to right, bring back to balanced position, then tip to left, front, and back.

Child should stand on twist board on tiptoes.

Have child stand on twist board, twist right to left and left to right. Ask for variations.

Have child stand on twist board continually to right, going in a complete circle.

Have child stand on twist board while in a squatting position.

BODY AWARENESS ACTIVITIES

Children need to experiment with the usage of both sides of the body. In many children the difference between the two sides of the body has not been established, because of emphasis being placed upon using the preferred side. We believe that because the body is designed symmetrically, both sides of the body should be developed in order to achieve greatest efficiency.

Have children lie on floor and try to make circles in the air with their feet.

Have children lie on back, slide arms slowly overhead until they touch. Return.

Have children lie on back, slide legs apart slowly. Return.

Have children lie on back, slide arms up, clap hands. Look toward hands when they clap.

Have children lie on back, slide right arm up, and left leg out. Reverse slide left arm up and right leg out. Slowly!

Have children stand and draw circles and lines with fingers and hands: (1) in front, (2) overhead, (3) point to floor, (4) behind them, (5) to the side of them.

Encourage variations and "another way" for each of the activities.

Angels in the snow—have children slide both arms and both legs up and back.

The teacher should ask the child to:

Draw own self

Collect pictures of specific parts of the body. Make a scrapbook

Imitate the movement of a specific part. Always identify the part

Explore the different ways a body part can move (hand clapping, tapping, shaking, clicking, and so forth)

Experiment with body parts in front of a mirror

Supply the name after usage of a part has been stated

Lying on the floor with eyes closed, touch specific body parts that are named

Use body parts with his surroundings (touch table with nose, wall with back, floor with knees)

Bat a balloon with a specified part of his body

Use parts of his body to propel objects through space (kick a ball, catch a ball, pull a wagon)

The teacher should cut up paper dolls and put each into a separate envelope. Distribute to children and ask them to reassemble the person. Interpret the movement of each part as it is put together.

Play games: Looby-lou, Simon says, Hokey pokey, Look, see, I can do this, See what I can do, Did you ever see a lassie

The teacher should challenge the child to move toward:

The front

The back

To the left side

To the right side

The ceiling

The floor

To the sides of the room

To the corner of the room

The top and bottom of objects in the room

Around the objects in the room with front, side, and back facing objects

Challenge spatial awareness by:

Setting up a varied obstacle course including something to crawl through, go under, over, squeeze through, runaround

Encouraging creative movement using any equipment in the room. Use the child's imagination and creativity. *Do not demonstrate!* Have children move around among each other and change speeds, levels, and directions

Challenge creative movement by asking the children to:

Be a tree

Show me how tall you can be

Show me how small you can be

Show me how wide you can be

Show me how tall and thin you can be

Make yourself small again. What do you look like? (ball) Roll like a ball

Point to the farthest wall. Touch it and come back to your own space.

Point to the nearest wall. Run to it and back to your own space without touching anything

Standing in your own place, make your feet move fast

Standing in your own place, make your feet move slowly

Activities that a child may explore on a mat:

Rolling like a log

Crawling (forward and backward)

Walking on knees

Playing like combat (crawl on stomach)

Scoot on back, push with feet

Forward roll

Backward roll

Walking on hands and feet

Crab walk

Twisting in different shapes

Working with a partner in the above activities

Creating combinations of the above activities

There are many excellent books that will provide additional activities for children in movement and dance. Two such resources are *Physical Education for Today's Boys and Girls*[2] and *Learning through Movement: Developmental and Conceptual Approach.*[3]

REFERENCES

1. Cratty, Bryant J., and Martin, Sister Mary: Perceptual-motor efficiency in children, Philadelphia, 1969, Lea & Febiger.
2. Andrews, Gladys, Saurborn, Jeanette, and Schneider, Elsa: Physical education for today's boys and girls, Boston, 1960, Allyn & Bacon, Inc.
3. Yates, Tommy C.: Learning through movement: developmental and conceptual approach, Lafayette, Ga., 1974, Northwest Georgia Cooperative Educational Services Agency.

chapter 6

Design for perceptual-motor learning

The conventional definition of perceptual-motor response incorporates the three processes of discrimination and input, integration with past experiences, and purposeful movement in a motor response. (Often a monitoring of the response is purposed as a fourth element.) (Fig. 6-1.)

PURPOSES OF PERCEPTUAL-MOTOR ACTIVITIES

Since it has been established that perception arises from sensory experience, experimenters have accepted the explanation that sensory experience was the prime factor in size and depth perception.

Developing that thought we find that perceptual-motor experiences rely on sensory input for integration and response. Logically then, it would follow that the more experiences, the richer the development. Input and discrimination occur as a pattern of nervous impulses are sent to the individual's brain where integration takes place. Integration is a process by which the individual uses past experiences to perceive what response is indicated. Therefore, we might say that the input has meaning for the individual. A translation of the input occurs and the output is generated, in this case, a motor response. If the child has no interpretation or meaning attached to the input, perception will be inadequate and an inaccurate response will probably result. In the case of a perceptual-motor response, the innervation

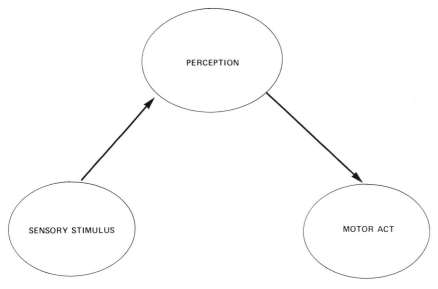

Fig. 6-1

to the muscle will be inappropriate resulting in a faulty motor response to the sensory stimulus.

Many perceptual-motor specialists say that a monitoring system in the translation process acts as a feedback situation and can alter the response if it seems inappropriate for the situation. This continuous monitoring acts as a gauge until a correct response occurs.

This is a simple explanation for a very complex process with many influencing factors. It is important, however, for the basic process to be understood by the teacher of the young child.

Some signs that may indicate perceptual-motor deficiencies readily observable by the teacher of the young child are the following:

1. Lack of coordination in motor skills
2. Clumsiness in daily activities
3. Difficulty in coloring large symbols
4. Difficulty in matching symbols and shapes
5. Constant inattentiveness
6. Consistent short attention span
7. Inability to recognize and interpret symbols correctly
8. Inability to interpret pictures correctly
9. Difficulty with letter and number sequences

10. Inability to reproduce letters, numbers and symbols correctly
11. Difficulty in form and depth perception
12. Difficulty in interpreting lateral directions
13. Short retention duration
14. Lack of consistent dominance
15. Poor self-concept
16. Lack of desire for participation in games
17. Poor performance in movement and dance activities
18. Inability to name body parts

The following gross motor activities will enhance the child's ability to perceive and to produce an adequate motor response.

Perceptual-motor activities include both fine motor and gross motor responses, but in this book we will include only gross motor responses. Concentration will be on those activities that include balance, agility, coordination, flexibility, strength, speed, and endurance motor skills and could enhance the development of intelligence, reading skills, and concept formation. Let's take an example from Boorman[1] on integration with language arts. Here the child wrote the poem, and interpreted it through dance movements.

THE FOREST FIRE

It sparkles and crackles, and pops and burnings,
that's what the forest fire does.
It hunts and kills the hills,
that's what the forest fire does.
                                    —Rob S. Merrill, Grade 3[2]

We have a great deal of evidence that success in physical skills contributes to enhanced self-concept and positive reinforcement of self-image.[3] Your own experiences will support this also. Children who experience success, joy, excitement, and fulfillment from moving and playing are receiving immediate positive reinforcement.

Figs. 6-2 to 6-4, give the results of a 3-week experiment in perceptual-motor activities with second grade children. The pictures drawn by the children afterward show that they were able to draw a better idea of their body form and image. In all three cases, better representation of the body parts were evident. Melvin discovered his shoulders, feet, and five fingers; Tony had more accurate color, dimensions, and scale; and Sean became more aware of his neck, shoulders, and dimensions.

Hedges and Hardin, based on a study in Missouri, said,

*The child whose perceptual skills have been de-
veloped and extended is the child who is free to
profit from instruction and to learn indepen-
dently. The greater the development of perceptual skills, the greater the capacity for making learning effective.*[4]

Perceptual-motor development is currently receiving much discussion
as one of the correlates of readiness for reading as well as for academic
achievement.

The total organic and developmental approach characterized by theo-
reticians such as Piaget has shown tendency to look at reading as one part
of a larger perceptual-motor response to environment and at failure to
achieve mastery in differentiating the visual symbols of the printed page
as potentially a part of perceptual immaturity.

Kephart[5] believed that the ability to deal with symbolic and conceptual
materials was based upon consistent and true perceptions of the environment. Kindergarten children with limited perceptual experiences are more
likely to encounter difficulties with reading than those who have had adequate perceptual experiences.

Perceptual-motor activities in the elementary school curriculum can be
of value in remediation, enrichment, enhancement, and motivation. They
offer another dimensional interpretation to expression and communication
and the learning of form and symbol interpretation. In preschool age children it can be viewed as preventive.

The optimum time to preclude difficulties in perceptual-motor learning
would be during the preschool stages.

The message is quite simple; the more stimulation the child receives,
the greater the perception he achieves, whatever the modality. He becomes
a fuller, richer person—more complete, higher coping quotient, and greater
dimensions are achieved in learning and in living. The motor dimension
contributes its fair share to the total development and is in itself its own
justification for inclusion.

SELF-EXPRESSION ACTIVITIES

Telling about yourself without words. What do you like to do with
your friends? Show me. (Children may offer the following through movements.)

Row a boat
Ride a bicycle
Play with a ball

Fig. 6-2

Fig. 6-2, cont'd

Fig. 6-3

Fig. 6-3, cont'd

Fly a kite
Walk on the beach
Play in the sand
Swim
Swing
Slide down a slide
Visit a zoo
Go to the store
Can you tell a story through movement? Use different signs and movements to tell us what you want us to know.
What did you do after school?
Where did you go last weekend?
How did you feel coming to school this morning?
Can you draw yourself today? What colors are you wearing?
Draw your hands. What do they do?
Draw your feet. What do they do?
Draw your eyes. What do they do?
Draw your legs and arms. What do they do?

Fig. 6-4

Post test

Fig. 6-4, cont'd

Fig. 6-5

Tell how you are different from others by the way you move.
How do you walk?
How do you run?
What can you do with your body?
How do you move at home?
How do you move at school?
What can you do that no one else can?
Can you tell us what kind of movements you can do?
What are fast movements? Show us.
What are big movements? Show us.
What are movements which are hard to do? Show us.
What are easy movements? Show us.

What are round movements? Show us.

What are slow movements? Show us.

What are up and down movements? Show us.

What are soft movements? Show us.

What are spinning movements? Show us.

Can you move to music?

Can you go up and down with the music? Show us.

Can you go around with the music? Show us.

Can you go fast with the music? Show us.

Can you go slowly with the music? Show us.

Can you go low and high with the music? Show us.

Can you dance with the music?

Can you dance like a leaf falling? Show us.

Can you dance like a tree swaying? Show us.

Can you dance like a top? Show us.

Can you dance like a bird flies? Show us.

Can you dance like fire burns? Show us.

Can you dance like ocean waves? Show us.

Can you think of another way that only you can dance? Show us.

FORM PERCEPTION

The recognition of symbols and forms is of utmost importance to a child in today's educational system. Indeed life may depend on his recognition of signs or colors as he walks to school each day. As the academic process begins, recognition of symbols is basic to all skills. Recognition of symbols requires the process of perception, which may be enhanced through perceptual-motor activities. Children may learn the concepts of space and shapes through movement expressions. The following activities are suggested for form discrimination learning of sizes, shapes, straight and curved lines, depth perception and figure-ground relationships (Fig. 6-6).

Draw geometric shapes on the playground. Have the children use the basic locomotor patterns to move from one shape to another.

Design the play area to include lines of different dimensions and with curves as well as straight lines. Have the children walk these lines at different levels, and with different speeds and directions.

Have the children make different shapes with their bodies.

Have the children throw fleece balls at various shapes and from different distances.

Fig. 6-6. (Courtesy Educational Facilities Laboratories, New York. Photograph by Ron Partridge.)

Have the children chose beanbags of different geometric shapes. Have them chose a different one each day.

Have the children cut out different shapes, and see how many ways they can move around that shape.

OCULAR TRACKING

Very young children need a great deal of practice in the development of controlled eye movements. Visual perceptions will be poorly developed without constant visually related experiences. Eye-hand coordination activities are essential, and in addition, ocular tracking activities should be planned. The following activities will offer tracking skills.

Suspend a whiffle ball by a string, and ask the child to touch it with one finger when it comes to him

Swing the suspended ball from side to side and ask the child to keep his finger with the ball, as it swings

Fig. 6-7

Have the child hit a large thrown object
Have the child strike the suspended ball with his hand
Have the child trace a line on the wall from left to right
Have the child trace a series of geometric shapes with fingers
Have the child catch different types and size of objects with a scoop
Have the child hit different objects with a paddle
Have the child watch a tennis match
Have the child play television table tennis

Fig. 6-8

PERCEPTUAL-MOTOR TESTS

Bender Visual Motor Gestalt Test for Children
Set of Cards $2.50; 25 Record Forms $5.50; Manual $6.00
> The Psychological Corporation
> 304 East 45th Street
> New York, New York 10017

Bingham Button Test
> Kindergarten Office
> Annie Lytle School
> Jacksonville, Florida

Gesell Developmental Examination
Ilg and Ames Test Materials and Recording Sheets to accompany *School Readiness* by Frances L. Ilg and Louise Bates Ames $4.00

> Harper & Row, Publishers
> New York, New York

Illinois Test of Psycholinguistic Abilities
Complete Examiner's Kit of Testing Materials $32.00

> University of Illinois Press
> Urbana, Illinois

Learning Methods Test
Robert Mills. Set of complete manual of directions, a pad of 25 record forms, and a box of 420 picture word cards—40 of which are used during the test administration $6.00

> The Mills Center
> 1512 East Broward Boulevard
> Fort Lauderdale, Florida

Marianne Frostig Developmental Test of Visual Perception
Test Specimen set $5.00; Examiners Kit $10.50; Set of 25 Tests $11.00; Scoring Manual $3.00

> Follett Publishing Company
> 1010 West Washington Boulevard
> Chicago, Illinois 60607

Psychoeducational Inventory of Basic Learning Abilities
Robert E. Valett. Manual $12.00; Student Workbooks—set of 25 $10.50

> Fearon Publishers
> 6 Davis Drive
> Belmont, California 94002

Purdue Perceptual-Motor Survey
Eugene G. Roach and Newell C. Kephart. Manual $3.95; Package of 25 cards $1.00; Surveys $3.95

> Charles E. Merrill Publishing Company
> 300 Alum Creed Drive
> Columbus, Ohio 43216

Shape-O-Bay Test
> Jerry Thomas
> Florida State University
> Tallahassee, Florida

Winter Haven, Perceptual Copy Forms and Incomplete Copy Forms
> Winter Haven Lions Research Foundation
> Box 1045
> Winter Haven, Florida

REFERENCES

1. Boorman, Joyce: Dance and language experiences with children, Don Mills, Ontario, 1973, Longman Canada Limited.
2. Ibid., p. 6.
3. Rowen, Betty: The children we see, New York, 1973, Holt, Rinehart and Winston, Inc.
4. Hedges, William D., and Hardin, Veralee B.: Effects of a perceptual-motor program on achievement of first graders, Educational Leadership, ASCD, Washington, D.C. **30:**249, 1972.
5. Godfrey, Barbara B., and Kephart, Newell C.: Movement patterns and motor education, New York, 1969, Appleton-Century-Crofts, p. 4.

chapter 7

Teaching strategies for motor development

Movement education for very young children can consist of free play in a guided, environmentally designed play area and planned activities in a learning setting (Fig. 7-1).

The free play should take place several times during the day with guided supervision and the children should be encouraged to explore and engage in vigorous activities of their own choice. The play areas should be designed to facilitate perceptual-motor activities, and to provide challenges for motor development. The free play periods should be long enough to allow the child enough time for sufficient pursuit of endurance and strength building activities in a variety of situations.

During the supervised free play periods the teacher has the opportunity to diagnose the child's abilities and to note the quality of his skills. This diagnosis requires a thorough knowledge of efficient motor patterns, and the analysis of these movements. It will not be helpful to know that the child cannot jump over an object unless something is known about correcting the inadequacy. Usually, the young child should be challenged by increased environmental stimuli rather than directed by instruction in the development stages of motor patterns. Guided correction may be necessary if the basic pattern has been formed incorrectly.

Observing the child in free play serves to identify needed objectives for

Fig. 7-1. (Courtesy Educational Facilities Laboratories, New York. Photograph by Ron Partridge.)

the guided, formal learning periods. In the formal learning periods, a child should be challenged with movement tasks designed to improve his motor development at his own stage of readiness. With young children, the arrangement of equipment and materials plays an important part in this challenge. Often, it is essential only to suggest that the child "throw as far as he can" or to "jump over an object" to elicit the correct pattern response. Children at a preliterate age do not respond well to directed, verbal instruction. Demonstration often becomes an elimination factor because the child cannot perform the pattern correctly and is therefore forced into a failure situation. It would be better to allow the child to evolve the correct pattern through purposeful, planned objectives using challenging equipment and tasks than to force the child into an adult pattern before his motor readiness has developed. The problem-solving approach provides for this type of learning response.

Because the program is structured around individual differences, it is best to evaluate its effectiveness in terms of its value as a self-motivating program.

It is a useful teaching method because very little explanation is necessary to get the children to begin participating, and it allows maximum time for activity. Moreover, discipline is not a problem because every child is actively involved.

In addition, the teacher has an opportunity to give guidance while the child is working. For example, "How many ways can you move on your feet? Can you find another way? Could you make a different shape? Could you change direction? How?"

Most important to us as teachers is the fact that it allows us to give each individual child specific guidance in regard to his needs with the kind of activity or skill that that particular child would be most apt to do successfully. Through a better understanding of his abilities and weaknesses, self-concept and self-realization can be further developed.

This program also presents us with the opportunity to view firsthand those children who have particular problems, to assess their needs, and to prescribe the movement that would best enrich their lives.

LEARNING THROUGH ENVIRONMENTAL DESIGN

Teaching strategies for young children should always begin by the setting up of a learning environment that stimulates many movement possibilities (Fig. 7-2). The teacher should provide constant moral support and become an encouragement figure in the movement atmosphere. The child should be challenged with open-ended challenges that are success oriented. The challenges should allow for varied responses, all within the framework of acceptability. As the child achieves success, he will become more confident of the ability to handle the body in movement situations. The child will begin to pursue more demanding movement tasks. At this point, the teacher should allow the child to attempt activities that seem to be hazardous without commenting. Fearful utterances from a teacher will undermine the self-confidence of the child, and will, in many cases cause an accident. As long as the child initiates the action task, he will feel confident in his ability to pursue it, and will in most cases be extremely successful in his efforts, no matter how ambitious the movement. Many times teachers unwittingly instill fear of heights by suggesting that the child "might fall." The child, feeling that this is obviously not pleasing the teacher, promptly falls, since that was

Fig. 7-2. (Courtesy Educational Facilities Laboratories, New York. Photograph by Ron Partridge.)

her suggestion. Adult interpretations of the young child's ability are often tinged with "memory fear" of one's own limitations. Children have a great deal of self-confidence in their own motor ability and if allowed to pursue activities can become amazingly adept at a very young age.

As the child begins to solidify a basic pattern, care should be taken through analysis of that pattern to see that it forms correctly for the greatest proficiency. Formative stages of development are occurring at 2 to 5 years of age in most children and care should be exercised to make sure that the child does not go beyond that age with an immature motor pattern. Observation, analysis, and diagnosis of the child's movements are very important in those formative stages. Once the pattern has been formed incorrectly, remedial teaching is indicated but may not be successful in stimulating optimum development.

The opportunity should be provided for the child to practice his skills. Repeated practice will increase self-confidence and stabilize basic skills. In addition, the child should be encouraged to use his skills in a variety of movement activities. The more practice the child gets in different ways, the better skilled he will be. Practice is the most important variable in the learning of motor skills.

The components of movement based on motor development facts should be the basis for the selection of skills for a particular age level. Recognizing that all children do not grow and develop at the same rate, the individual basis within each lesson will provide a comprehensive range of movement patterns. Therefore, each child will not be subjected to planned, rigid skill patterns, with adult expectations of achievement, but instead those based on their own readiness level. Good class procedure will provide for the handicapped, the obese, the skilled, and the average. A well-organized play experience can challenge each child to his optimum potential and offer physical rewards for all. Quality movement can be assured, just as quality learning is assured in other domains.

Let us think in terms of skill progression from infancy. The child first learns to grasp, to climb, to crawl, and to walk. These stages are fairly well established, but each child will not achieve these stages at the same age. Why then should they be expected to achieve subsequent skills at the same age?

Physical educators have, through the years, planned games for children, games for preschool, or games for primary grades. Provision has been made for the group rather than the individual and it has been based on watered-down junior high school curriculum. It has been known that learning takes palce in the situation where the development of any skill is commensurate with the individual's ability. Although games are based on the basic skills, they are structured, patterened movements with many factors that a child must master in order to excel. Children who have had very little previous exposure to skill acquisitions, who do not possess the readiness factor, or who may be handicapped in some respect, are penalized. It is important to include *all the children in all the activities*. We must assume, still bearing in mind the individual child, that what is good for one child is good for all children. After all, fundamental motor skills relate to all life activities, not just games. Experience has shown that when children have a chance at physical activity, going to school is more of a joy, and learning is easier. The mind and body receive excellent training through response to action directions, and through response to self-directed problem solving (Fig. 7-3).

Teachers should have a knowledge of the movement skills, and their relative good form. It is not enough to provide the situation for move-

Fig. 7-3

ment training; it must be properly directed as well. This does not mean that the teacher should explain the correct form, but rather encourage the individual in the achievement of his own movements. A teacher would not expect rote learning in other subjects; therefore, why movement education or physical education? Let us treat the basic movement skills as any other developmental skill.

LEARNING THROUGH MOVEMENT EXPLORATION

In early childhood, movement exploration can be defined as using guided play as a learning experience rather than as recreation or amusement. Much of a child's daily life is spent in play activities. Adults spend a great deal of their efforts toward encouraging play but usually the objective is to amuse the child. However, child learning centers are now challenging the child in active pursuits, even though they have often been reluctant to set up equipment for gross motor experiences because of accidents. They know that movement experiences can be used as an educational tool because of these factors:

Children engage in movement activities readily

Children enjoy movement activities

Children need activity for growth and development

Children gain self-confidence through movement

Teachers using movement exploration with young children should include activities for motor development in three and possibly four levels of psychomotor taxonomy.

Examples are:

Activities that allow learning at one's own rate

Activities in which all children can participate

Activities that challenge a child at his own level of progression

Activities that allow each child to be responsible for his own perception and response (self-expression)

Activities that allow exploration and creativity

Activities that allow rhythmic responses

Activities that allow natural movements to become refined through guided discovery—not forced

Activities that incorporate psychomotor components, relationships, body handling skills, gross motor, fine motor responses

Activities that allow natural progression in skill acquisition

Environments that are safe, child-centered, and challenging (made by children for children)

The activities should be taught in:

Directed and nondirected teaching

Environmentally stimulated learning activities

Child-made environment as opposed to adult environment

Child-inspired progression and challenge

Natural evolution of finesse through practice exposure

Equipment stimulated activity

Peer relationships challenge (boys and girls the same)

Carefully planned activities with these components; verbal, nonverbal, dramatic, environmetal as appropriate to learning level

USING MOVEMENT IN CONCEPT FORMATION

Many key concepts can be learned by the child through the use of movement as a learning modality. Concepts in general academic studies can be learned through movement activities. The child's cognitive retention and effective behavior may be enhanced by reinforcement in the psychomotor domain. A child's communication of these concepts can often be expressed best through movement. The cognitive process includes perception, conceptualization, and practice or development and enrichment. Movement enhances this process by providing another dimension of stimuli.

Movement is an excellent motivator for tedious learning of concepts when the child may not want to pursue the activity. Motivation in mathematics may occur through manipulative activities, partner tasks and responses, and group problem-solving tasks and supported through the use of beanbags, targets, geometric mobiles, and other equipment. The equipment should be made with numbers, geometric symbols, and shapes. One example of how this can be done is to construct a target with geometric designs of different colors and labeled with letters or numbers. Attach a small plastic ball by a string to the back of the cardboard. The string can be adjusted to various lengths according to the aptitude of the child. The child is then challenged to grasp the ball, step back to the end of the string, and throw the ball at the target. The target selection can be given in task by the teacher or announced as a "goal" by the child.

Symbolic expression through movement can help with reading skills when the problem-solving tasks are given in written or symbolic form. The child reads the cue to perform the next activity.

Musical concepts are natural combinations with movement and establish rhythmic communication. Children enjoy being half notes, whole notes, quarter notes, and forming musical phrases through action.

Examples of each of these multidisciplinary learnings are included on the following pages.

CONCEPT LEARNING
Interpretation of symbols

Symbol recognition and interpretation can be facilitated through the following activities:

Using stick figure drawings of various sizes, have the children perform the movement as they perceive it—music may be used to encourage repetition of the movements—a march, for example, would encourage walking from the drawing of a step forward.

LEARNING THROUGH DANCE ACTIVITIES

The young child needs experiences in creative and interpretive communication through movement. The dance experience integrated into the child's learning experiences will offer avenues for this kind of expression.

The very young child needs to know how it "feels" to be joyous and to move joyously; to be sad and to depict that mood through movement expression. Many other feelings can be expressed through movement adding another dimension to the child's form of communication, such as happiness, light-heartedness and so forth.

These emotion-motivated movements can allow overt expressions of pent-up feelings through the totally developing dance experience. Self-concept, self-realization, and confidence may be obtained through this movement experience which offers the opportunity (1) to move, (2) to learn through moving, (3) to be creative through moving, (4) to learn rhythmic patterns of movement, (5) to develop confidence in handling the body in various space relationships, (6) to learn basic dance patterns, and (7) to combine movement activities with music, art, sicence, mathematics, and language arts.[1]

All of these and more can be obtained through the dance experience. How can we deprive our young children of these educational experiences that offer learning in each step of the psychomotor domain and include the most relevant learning environment for the nondiscursive area.

Sample movement lessons: 5-year-old-children

Lesson I

Place a circle (one foot by one foot) for each child on the movement area before the children arrive. Begin the lesson with the task "find a circle for your own."

When the children arrive, encourage them to choose something to do.

Before beginning the lesson, have a prearranged signal for control (clapping hands, drum, "freeze"). Gain the attention of the children (only briefly in order that they do not get restless).

Give them (very enthusiastically) a task, such as the following:

Tasks

Jump around the circle. Jump over the circle in as many ways as possible.

Run back and forth around the circle. How else can you go around the circle?

Walk on the circle, being careful not to step off.

Lie down—reach as high as possible.

Reach in every direction—make a wide cross with your arms— stretch another way—try another way.

While they are working, give each child a beanbag. Allow free play. Have them remain in circles. (This instills the idea of space.)

Ask, "What can you do with your beanbag?" Encourage advanced children to throw higher; catch with one hand; walk around while throwing and catching. Assist and encourage those having difficulty.

Allow each child to pursue the skills at his own level of achievement. Add challenges periodically to keep the superior child interested.

Have the children put away beanbags and return to circles. Have the children sit with backs straight, legs crossed in front. Have them breathe deeply and relax, several times. Review the words, the movements, and the objectives of the lesson.

Allow free play at the various movement centers. Move around and work with each child.

Lesson II

Preparation notes: Discuss the previous lesson with children. Ask questions about their movements.

Put a beanbag on the floor for each child, with plenty of space between beanbags. Use the entire movement area. (This is important.) Mark wall and floor targets. Send the children to the play area with the assignment, "Find a beanbag and a space for your own."

Have a pre-arranged signal for control. (Perhaps holding up the beanbag.)

After allowing ample time for free play, give the following lesson·

Tasks

Remove shoes. Pick up the beanbag with one foot. Change feet. Jump with the beanbag on one foot, change. Throw the beanbag into the air, catch it with foot. Change feet. Put the beanbag between ankles. Jump up and catch it with hands. Jump over beanbag.

Stretch the beanbag out in front of you. Put it between your legs. Put it out to the side. Hold it high over your head. Higher. Put it on your head, and walk around in a circle. Walk faster. Walk backwards. Jump up with the bag on your head, and catch it as it falls off. Try something else. What else can you do?

Divide the class into prearranged partners. Have two throwing the beanbags against a target on the wall. Have several partners throwing to targets on the floor. Have several partners throwing to each other. Rotate the tasks. Have the children put the bean-bags on their heads, stand and relax. Finally have them walk with good posture, back to their own space.

Review the words, movements and objectives. Allow free play.

Lesson III

Discuss the previous lesson. Reemphasize the idea of working in a space. Review some the the skills attempted with the beanbag. Discuss a control signal.

Ask each child to find an object and jump over it. (Symbols and geometric designs may be marked on the outside play area, or with chalk on the inside area.)

Put enough balls (playground size) for each child in cardboard boxes at the play area. (Do not let the children see them.) After giving ample time for free play, gain their attention (prearranged signal) and tell them to get a ball, and return to their space. Follow this immediately with a "dumping" of the boxes of balls. Allow each child to retrieve one ball, and return to a space. Allow time for excitement and free play. Gain their attention and give the following lesson:

Tasks

Bounce and catch the ball with both hands. Throw the ball up and catch it with both hands. Bounce with one hand.

Walk in circle, throw the ball up and catch with both hands. Walk in circle. Bounce with one hand.

Free play. How else can you play with the ball?

Have different obstacle courses, targets, and challenge areas for children. Encourage exploration. Have the children return to their space and review the movements, and the objectives.

Allow free play in the movement centers.

DANCE AND LANGUAGE EXPERIENCES FOR LEARNING

In planning for children's learning it is important to realize that we should not separate the developmental stages of the child's learning in our desire to teach music, art, movement, dance, mathematics, and so forth. It is important, therefore, to present these disciplines in such a manner so as to integrate them within the total learning process.

The disciplines of music, language arts, and dance are ideally suited for composite teaching. The following activities will form a foundation of experiences on which the creative teacher may build a curriculum of learning moments through movement and dance that will "teach" mathematics, music, art, and language arts.

Action words may be used to stimulate movements.

Sounds, such as made by percussion instruments, stimulate rhythmic movements.

Records are very useful for providing creative music for listening and interpreting with the body.

Pictures may be used to stimulate movement and dance interpretations.

Animal interpretations are motivators to movement, and music can be found that enhances the animal movements.

Clapping rhythmic phrases and putting the rhythm in the body can be used to introduce body parts and body awareness.

Songs are good movement and dance motivators.

Poetry and stories stimulate the small child to dance.

Activity scenes or seansonals imagery are effective movement stimulators.

Gladys Andrews Fleming states, "Today a new emphasis is emerging in dance for children. From community to community, dance is gaining prominence with offerings for preschool children, television programs, and teachers of dance and professionals going into the congested urban centers and camps to present various kinds of dance for children."[1]

REFERENCE

1. Fleming, Gladys Andrews, editor: Children's dance, Washington, D. C., 1973, American Association for Health, Physical Education and Recreation.

chapter 8

Management for learning through movement

PLANNING THE ENVIRONMENT

The components of movement according to development facts should be the basis for the selection of a movement-learning environment for a particular age level. Recognizing that all children do not grow and develop at the same rate, the individual basis within each learning session should provide a comprehensive range of movement patterns. No child should be subjected to planned, rigid movement patterns, with the expectations of achievement precluded. Good planning procedure will provide for the challenge and interest of all children. A well-organized play area can challenge each child, and offer enjoyable physical rewards for all. Achieving objectives can be assured.

Let us think in terms of motor development progression from infancy. The child first learns to grasp, to climb, to crawl, and to walk. These stages are fairly well established, but each child will not achieve these stages at the same age. It has been known that learning takes place in the situation where the development of any skill is commensurate with the individual's ability. Although games are based on the basic skills, they are structured, patterned movements that a child must master in order to excel. Children who have had very little previous exposure to skill acquisition, or who may be handicapped in some respect, are penalized. Therefore, it is important

93

to include all the children in the activities. Very young children do not need structured movement sessions.

Fundamental motor skills relate to all live activities, not just games. Experience has shown that when children have a chance at physical activity, without group pressure, participation is a joy, and management is less of a burden.

ORGANIZING THE LEARNING ENVIRONMENT

Children should be dressed for activity so that movement is not inhibited. This can be achieved with a minimum of effort. With parental support, children can be dressed appropriately on coming to the sessions. Happily, many children now dress for mobility. Shoes may be removed for better freedom and to enhance tactile input.

The program outlined for the preschool will be based on the use of equipment, and basic movement leading to overall motor development. In this program, each child must have his own space and equipment.

The use of the equipment will encourage the child to explore and to improve the progress individually; to gain eye-hand coordination skills with balloons, balls, with paddles and balls, bats and balls; to handle the body in relation to objects; and above all, to understand the body, how it moves—what it can do. The child will be building a vocabulary of movements, and will be moving, growing, and learning to adjust to this growth.

SAFETY

The hazards of play often tend to limit the liberties which teachers allow in movement lessons. One factor that should be considered is that *children will only attempt those feats in which they feel confident.* It follows, therefore, that in using the problem-solving technique, the child will provide his own limits. *Under no circumstances* should the teacher suggest *danger* to the child. Inspire confidence by giving encouragement for a daring performance.

The teacher *can* contribute to the safety of the lesson by being observant toward play area hazards. The area should be carefully inspected before each lesson, and all possible danger spots eliminated. Equipment should be inspected for breaks or splinters. Making a safe area is a very important part of the lesson planning.

The teacher should also be aware of each child's movements at all times during the lessons. Proper organization and control is essential to good movement training.

ORGANIZATIONAL CHECKLIST FOR MOVEMENT LESSON

1. Prepare review of previous lesson (such as a story).
2. Prepare daily objectives for proposed lesson.
3. Agree on a control signal with children (such as freeze).
4. Prepare alternate lesson for inclement weather (only where necessary).
5. Plan for utilization of space and learning centers.
6. Diagram area with marking and targets needed.
7. Plan for all needed equipment. (Be sure each child has equipment.)
8. Plan for equipment improvisation (where necessary).
9. Place equipment in area preceding arrival of children.
10. Make safety check.
11. Plan for activities to change with least possible confusion.
12. Arrange for helpers to bring in equipment and work with children.
13. Prepare a task for immediate absorption on arrival.
14. Plan how to get pupils to and from the play area.

FLOOR PLAN

In preparation for a movement lesson, make learning centers in the play space. This will situate each child 3 to 5 feet away from other children on all sides, and will provide him with plenty of space for exploring his own abilities. When the children enter the learning environment, allow each child to find a learning center and begin to explore. For the first several weeks it may be necessary to continually reinforce the importance of each child using his own learning center and apparatus.

The children should soon learn to relate to their space as a center of orientation, and around this idea the activities described in this chapter can be organized.

A definite value of this type of organization is that it gives opportunity for large or small group work. Once the different motor learning centers have been determined by the teacher, it is then possible to deal with challenges in individual ways.

The floor plan demonstrates how certain areas of the movement space can be used to work on different problem levels. One area can be used for balance work or mat work involving locomotion. Another area can be used for perceptual problems involving the tracking skills or eye-hand coordination. The remainder of the class can participate in various activities using the space for locomotor relationships.

MOVEMENT CENTERS
Indoor spaces

An indoor space for movement should be set up in an area where the child can enjoy it freely. It should contain equipment for eye-hand coordination and environmental stimuli such as balls and targets, fleece balls, goals, walls for rebounds and catching skills, beanbags, hoops and ropes, suspended balls, bats, and other manipulative objects. It should also include mats, climbing ropes, balance equipment, portable climbing equipment such as blocks and ladders, mirrors for children to observe their own movements, cubes, tubes, and other perceptually challenging equipment. All the equipment in the space should provide sensorimotor stimuli,

Fig. 8-1

that is, different textures, geometric designs, sound equipment, colors, and other stimulating motivators for purposeful action.

Outdoor space

Outdoor play space has often been designed to amuse chidlren, rather than to provide motor development learning experiences. Properly designed outdoor play centers should provide space to run freely with up and down hillsides and challenging obstacles for dodging and climbing over. Portable obstacles are preferred to fixed ones to enable the child to redesign the areas. Portable boxes, ladders, barrels, and planks will challenge creativity and child-centered design. Smooth, hard surfaces are essential to offer spaces to ride or push wheeled equipment and for bouncing balls. The hard surfaces should have adjacent flat walls for use with balls and paddles. Lines and targets in different colors may be painted on the hard surfaces.

Climbing, hanging, and crawling equipment should be installed on grassy areas and around the edges of the open spaces. A trampoline-like piece of equipment made from an old bed spring may be set up as a jumping pit in this area. Sand boxes, wading pools, and other small group activity centers may be added.

Trees are essential for climbing and for shade areas. They also provide a place for the child to sit and to observe the activities of other children from a different perspective.

Outdoor spaces can be very creatively designed to allow for flexibility of arrangement, especially if very few obstacles and equipment are fixed. Swings, slides, fixed "jungle gyms," and rocking horses are not recommended since they "move the children" rather than allowing the children to move themselves.

SPECIFIC EQUIPMENT: INDOOR-OUTDOOR
Equipment

Equipment for use in an early childhood movement education program can be made. Since large apparatus is the most expensive when purchased, methods of construction of indoor apparatus and a creative outdoor play are suggested. These ideas may serve as a motivator to creativity in developing one's own equipment.

Larger equipment

Climbing stairs—movable but not too steep
Rocking boat-stairs combination

Balance boards—2 × 4 inches × 10 feet with reversible bases
Planks and trestles (aluminum preferred)
Trampoline, innerspring mattress, large inner tubes covered with canvas
Climbing ropes, cargo nets
Wall targets, supended targets
Rebound throwing nets
Wooden blocks—12 × 12 × 12 inches, 4 × 4 × 12 inches, 24 × 8 × 8 inches
Variable speed phonograph (tempo control)
Tumbling mats or lightweight mattress
Plastic wading pool, sand box, jumping pits
Cardboard boxes
Percussion instruments
Movable saw horses
Movable planks and blocks
Push and pull objects
Ladders
Movable horizontal bars
Tunnels, boxes
Tires (various sizes)
Spools
Rubber utility balls
Plastic whiffle balls, baseball size
Plastic whiffle balls, softball size
Yarn balls, various sizes
Short plastic bats
Sponge rubber ball, 3 inch diameter, or used tennis balls
Frisbees (or sturdy paper plates)
Balloons
Beach balls
Hula hoops
Jump ropes
Chinese stretch ropes
1 inch wide flat strips of rubber tubes
Plastic detergent bottles (scoops)
Drum
Tambourine
Bamboo poles, various sizes from 3 to 8 feet long

Phonograph records
Wands of different colors
Milk cartons
Suspended balls
Walking beams, round and square

HOW TO MAKE SMALL APPARATUS EQUIPMENT
Hoops (Fig. 8-2)

Hoops for young children can be made from small garden hose ⅛ inch in diameter. Hose lengths may vary according to the age of the child:

Fig. 8-2

lengths of 24 to 30 inches are successful for preschool ages. The hose is cut and ends are joined with a dowel and stapled (tape should be used to cover the staples). It may be possible to join the ends over the dowel and have it hold without the use of the staples.

Large hoops can be made by cutting ¾-inch pipe into lengths 8⅓ feet long, fastening the ends together with dowel and heavy duty staples. This joint is then covered with electricians' tape.

Small hoops can be made from ⅜ inch garden hose cut into lengths of 54 inches and joined together with a 1½ inch piece of ⅜ inch dowel. Tape joining point.

Ring-toss hoops can be made the same way but cut into shorter lengths. Tape the joined edges.

Ring-toss target can be made using 1 inch thick board. Almost any size square can be used. Nail a 5½ or 6 inch piece of ¾ inch dowel to the center of the square, then paint (Fig. 8-3).

Tire maze

A series of tires are placed in the ground at varied heights and at different angles. The children walk on top of the tires, go over them in different ways, or crawl through them.

Balls

Preschool children start eye-hand activity with balloons or fleece or yarn balls. When the child progresses to playground balls, the 6- or 7-

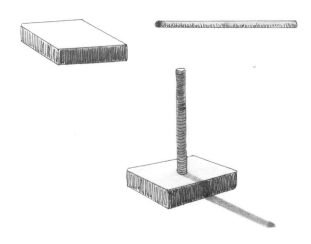

Fig. 8-3

inch ball is the easiest for this age to handle. It is important to expose the children to different size balls.

During the final phases of the movement program in preschool, children should be exposed to activity with basketballs, volleyballs, kickballs, and suspended balls. These are not the most important, however, and should not be purchased until other equipment is secured. These balls can often be obtained from the upper elementary physical education teachers.

The plastic ball in either softball or baseball size is a very usable item. These balls can be easily converted into suspended balls by tying sash cord through the holes. Tape should be used to reinforce the tying space.

Yarn balls (Fig. 8-4)

Place two cardboard circles with hole in the center, one on top of the other, and wind the yarn around cardboard, cut around edge, wrap and tie between cardboard, then cut and remove cardboard.

Another way to make a yarn ball is to cut a piece of cardboard approximately 4 inches long and about 2 inches wide. Wrap the yarn around the long side of the cardboard until it appears full. Slip the yarn off the cardboard and tie a piece of yarn around the center. Cut the looped ends and fluff.

Fig. 8-4

Beanbags (Fig. 8-5)

Cut material of different textures into various sizes and shapes, sew edges and fill with dried beans or corn, and close openings. Embroider numbers or letters on the outside of the bag after it is finished.

Scoops (Fig. 8-6)

Using empty, cleaned out bleach bottles, preferably ½- or 1-gallon bottles, cut the portion as shown and tape the edges.

Targets (Fig. 8-7)

Use cans. After they have been open and cleaned out, paint them different colors. When the paint has dried, tape the opened edge. They could also be numbered or lettered. They can be stacked and used as targets.

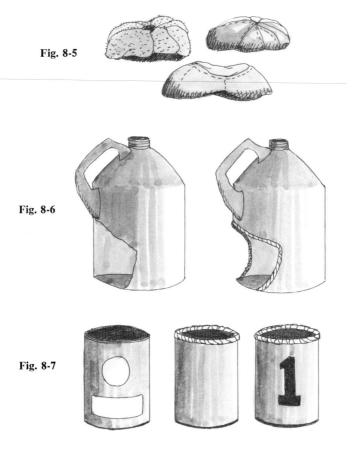

Fig. 8-5

Fig. 8-6

Fig. 8-7

Cup-ball game (Fig. 8-8)

For handle cut dowel stick into 5-inch lengths. Tack a plastic cup onto the handle but before you tack on completely, tie a piece of string or yarn around the tack, then tack together completely. Glue or use a needle to attach a small ball or fishing cork. The handles and balls can be painted.

Teetering boards (Fig. 8-9)

You need a block of wood that is 12 × 12 inches and you glue a half circle to the bottom of the block. When the glue has dried, also paint this one to make it more interesting for the children.

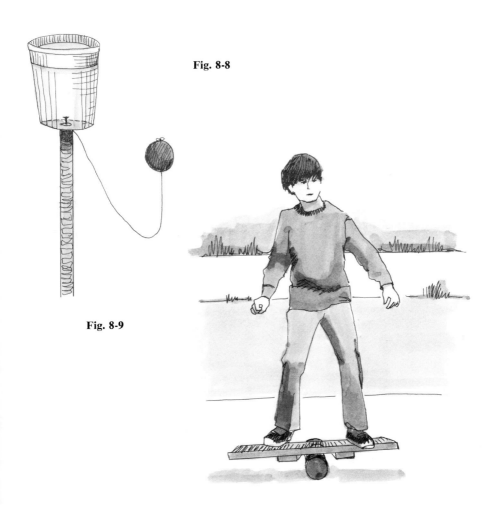

Fig. 8-8

Fig. 8-9

Ropes (Fig. 8-10)

The ropes are made by obtaining pieces of rope (the strength and texture to one's taste) and cutting them into an appropriate length, binding the raw edges with tape, so that they won't ravel. The tape also provides the children with a type of handle for holding.

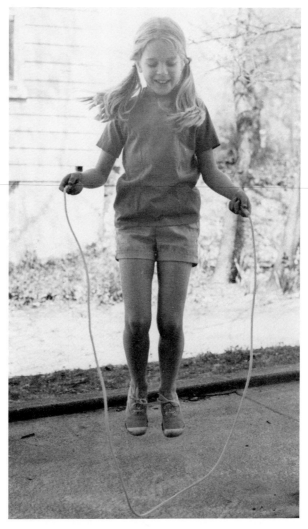

Fig. 8-10

Stilts (Fig. 8-11)

The tin can stilts are made by obtaining some large cans (such as those for juice) and removing the label. Tape around the edges to prevent the child from getting cut. Drill holes on opposite sides of the can and thread the rope through the can. Knot and then bind with tape to prevent it from coming apart. Paint may now be applied to the can and the stilts are ready to use.

Fig. 8-11

Climber (Fig. 8-12)

This piece of equipment is made from two saw horse type pieces with three cross bars in a line. These bars are drilled with holes into which several types of equipment may be fastened between the two. These include 4- by 4-inch beams, walking boards, spring boards, and parallel bars. Many variations are possible.

Hurdles (Fig. 8-13)

A simple way to make hurdles is to use cardboard boxes and yardsticks. Jump ropes may also be tied between traffic cones. A more versatile hurdle is made by drilling ½-inch holes at 8-inch intervals along a 4- by 4-inch board. The board is then cut into sections through the center of the holes. One-quarter inch dowels, 3 feet in length, are used for crossbars. Higher hurdles may be made by stacking. Two dowels may be used with four blocks to make a window effect for going through.

Tunnels (Fig. 8-14)

Tunnels can be constructed by bolting tires together and setting them in cement. Children may go over or through tunnels or they may jump from tunnel to tunnel.

Indoor-outdoor tunnels may be made from 55-gallon drums with both ends removed. Two are placed in frames at different heights and two are placed end to end in a low frame for a long tunnel.

Vertical ladder (Fig. 8-15)

Make the ladder in varied heights with varying distance between rungs.

Fig. 8-12

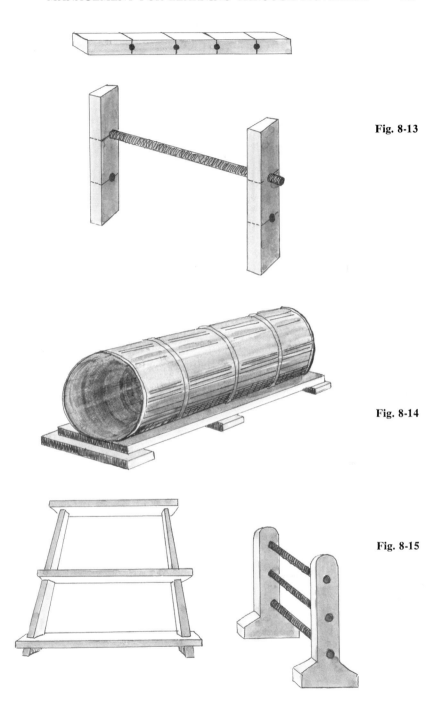

Fig. 8-13

Fig. 8-14

Fig. 8-15

Spinner

Cable spools are supported so that they may spin freely. Children try to walk on top of these or simply to balance in any way on them.

Spools

Various size cable spools are set in the ground at varied heights. The children move from spool to spool without touching. Different size spools are used so that children must control their bodies on different size areas while changing levels.

Towers

A series of cable spools are bolted together to form towers of various heights. The child may climb from tower to tower, jump from tower to tower, or from the towers to the ground.

Climbing apparatus

Supported from a tree, two ropes, a rope ladder, and a climbing pole are available for the children to use.

Climbing nets

The child experiences a sensation of free moving in all directions while climbing the net. Commercially built nets are available in several sizes.

Grip travel

An old swing set has been modified to support grip devices made from the ends of baseball bats.

Traveling rings

A 2- by 4-inch board is fastened between two trees. Traveling rings are supported from this.

Traveling tires

Small car tires are hung from a limb that is parallel to the ground. The children climb into, through, and from tire to tire.

Balance beams (Fig. 8-16)

The balance beam is the standard equipment in this area. Rather than use the commercial beam that is adjustable to a 2- or 4-inch width, it is more satisfactory to construct longer boards that are set permanently. By

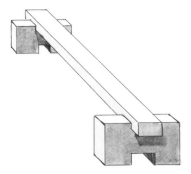

Fig. 8-16

using stools, balance beams may be raised to different heights. In addition, a more challenging course can be developed by using inclined, angled, and tapered beams.

Balance benches (Fig. 8-17)

The benches are constructed from 1- by 6-inch stock 8 feet in length. Benches both 10 inches and 20 inches high are used. The bench also has a 2-inch balance beam when turned upside down. The center supports are used to step through when the bench is laid on its side. The benches may be bolted together in a step pattern or "log cabin" design.

Used with the vertical ladders, inclines of different angles may be set up as well as setting the bench up to 3 feet off the ground.

Individual mats

If all children are to work on balance activities at the same time, it is important to have individual mats. A heavy rug may be cut into sections 3 by 4 feet and serve well for this purpose. Some sections both larger and smaller may be cut to add variety in work space.

Rocking boards, teeter boards, and roller-rollers

These are used both separately and with ball activities. The children also may work individually or in groups.

Tire patterns

Both car tires and bicycle tires are used to set patterns on the floor. The child can be given specific directions in using the patterns that require balance on either one or both feet or on some other part of the body.

Fig. 8-17

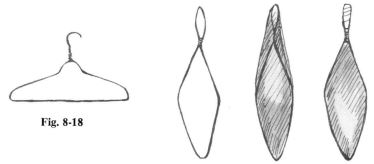

Fig. 8-18

Trampolines

Not the trampoline as usually thought of but rather large inner tubes either placed on mats or used on the grass is the trampoline of the kindergarten level. In addition, bounce boards may be constructed from 1- by 6-inch stock fastened to rounded 4- by 4-inch or 2- by 4- inch boards.

Fig. 8-19

Horses

Horses are primarily used to help pupils with upside-down balance. Horses are very useful but are time-consuming and fairly expensive to construct.

Targets

Targets should be meaningful to the child. Animal faces and clown faces are popular. Colors, shapes, and suspended targets are also well liked by small children.

Bats (Fig. 8-18)

A safe and inexpensive bat may be made for kindergarten children by bending a coat hanger into the desired shape and covering it with an old stocking, taping the handle and edges. Different color tape may be used. Support hose offers great resiliency.

Small yarn balls may be made for use with the bats or fleece balls, or may be purchased. Fleece balls are commercially prepared, but can be easily made.

chapter 9

Educational implications

The what, where, how, and why of movement with specific rationale have been discussed. In this chapter we want to explore the "why not" of movement, in relation to its educational implications. The developmental stages of children have been outlined by many. One of the most popular recent theorists, Piaget,[1] has given great validity to his conclusions and in fact has been widely accepted. If we take his basic stages and apply them to our concept of learning through movement, we find that they are compatible. Piaget states that the child uses movement and practice (play) to learn prior to conceptualizing or internalizing a "schema" or pattern of thought in the development of the intellect. He cites that the general age for this sensorimotor developmental stage is between 2 and 4 years of age. That is consistent with our basic premise that the young child learns through movement at preschool ages, and supports the claim that in fact it is the optimum time to encourage learning by using movement activities. Some child development specialists maintain that once a stage of learning has been passed without development occurring to its fullest, the child will be retarded in development in some way unless that stage is returned to, and remediated. Delacato[2] is a leading proponent of this theory. Following this thought, Kephart[3] believed in the essential part that movement played in the remediation of individuals who were handicapped.

If all these ideas or, in fact, empiricals have shown that children need movement for the development of the intellect (Piaget), in the development of a "normal" child (Delacato), and in the remediation of deviations (Kephart), then the inclusion of movement in the curriculum of the young child (1 to 5) has considerable merit.

Research cited in Chapter 2 indicated that children have the ability to perform many more movements than adults believed before cinematography. In my study of preschool-age children, pictorial comparisons proved that young children of 2, 3, 4, and 5 years of age could perform the basic movement patterns of kicking, throwing, striking, and jumping in a manner that resembled a mature performer's.[4] Studies by Wickstrom[5] and Halverson[6] have shown that basic patterns are well developed in young children, both boys and girls. All of the studies show that there is very little difference in the motor abilities of boys and girls at the 1- to 4-year-old level of development.

Around 5 years of age and thereafter, differences began to appear in relation to gross motor activities. The boys appeared to be more proficient in throwing and striking and the girls in jumping and kicking. This trend continued and was shown in Hanson's study with elementary age children.[7]

Practice seems to be another important variable. It is possible that it may be the one most important factor in the attainment of motor skill. For example, boys are generally more adept at physical activities than girls. This may be due to active versus passive pursuits in early childhood that are culturally induced. The "athletes" have always been active. The girl athletes today were the "tomboys" of yesterday. It is important to realize that they learned their skills at a very early age by practicing with peer groups, or with a very interested parent. They were not "taught" in formal classes in the main; they learned through participation.

If these observations about the motor skills of young children are true, planning for a variety of movement activities for young children between the ages of 1 and 5 will produce better physical skills in all children, not just the "little athletes" who are mostly boys.

Another reason for including movement activities as learning strategies is that they are a self-motivating enhancement to the development of self-concept. Many young children are reluctant to participate in any activity in which an adult is not leading. Many children have been overprotected and restricted. Many have learned to fear activity because an adult has instilled a fearful attitude toward play, especially in relation to heights. Through a well-planned program of movement activities, such children can overcome their hesitancy and achieve the self-realization that they can do all the things that other children can. They become confident and self-reliant. For example, one 2-year-old child would not leave his mother on arrival to the day care center. Finally after traumatic separation and departure of the mother the child would not leave the teacher, but would cling to her hand and cry violently on release. This went on for days. Finally the child began to watch the other children in their movement program and to hear the happy sounds and see the apparent joy that was experienced by the children. After a few days, the child ventured out to retrieve a ball. After reluctantly giving it up, the child did not reach for the teacher's hand immediately, but watched the ball longingly. The next day, the child came out with the teacher, left her, and joined the other children. (No special attention was given to him.) He participated every day therafter, began to achieve a great deal of success, and with it came confidence. After 2 weeks in the movement program, the child happily said goodbye to the mother and participated in all of the activities of the children's center. After 1 month in the program, the child displayed an entirely new self-concept. He was self-assured in activity, and in all group work and play at the center.

Physical educators and reading specialists have recently shown that participation in basic motor activities and in perceptual-motor activities have improved the reading skills of elementary age children. If movement activities can remediate, they can prevent; therefore there is perhaps another justification for their inclusion, that of preventing reading difficulties.

Rowen, in her book *The Children We See,* provides an excellent basis for observational study of the young child with case studies for reference. For the student who wishes to pursue child observation, it provides all the tools and the motive.

There are many other studies that could be cited and implications that could be drawn, but it is only important here to convince the person working with young children to try this type of learning modality. After experiencing the joy a child derives from participation, and the subsequent develoment that takes place in the total child as a result of a well-planned and well-taught program of movement activities, no futher justification will be necessary.

REFERENCES

1. Piaget, Jean: The origin of intelligence in children, New York, 1936, New York University Press, pp. 157-268.
2. Delacato, Carl: The diagnosis and treatment of speech and reading problems, Springfield, Ill., 1963, Charles C Thomas, Publisher.

3. Kephart, Newell E.: The slow learner in the classroom, Columbus, Ohio, 1960, Charles E. Merrill Publishing Co.
4. Flinchum, Betty M.: Selected motor patterns of preschool age children, Ph.D. dissertation, Louisiana State University, 1971.
5. Wickstrom, Ralph L.: Fundamental motor patterns, Philadelphia, 1970, Lea & Febiger.
6. Halverson, Lolas E.: Development of motor patterns in young children, Quest **6:** 44-53, 1969.
7. Hanson, Margie R.: Motor performance testing of elementary age children, Unpublished doctoral dissertation, University of Washington, Seattle, 1965.

Motor ability test

THIRTY-FIVE YARD DASH

Equipment:
    One measuring tape
    One stopwatch
    One set of footprints behind starting line
    Starting line and finish line
Administrators:
    One director
    One timer
    One scorer
    One assistant to "catch" the children
Number of trials:
    One trial
Directions:
    "Do you think you could run very fast this morning? Can you see Miss White? I want you to run to Miss White as fast as you can when I say 'run.' Miss White will catch you. Ready, run."
Scoring:
    Number of seconds

THROW—ACCURACY

Equipment:
    One set of footprints behind throwing line

117

Four targets 9 inches in diameter, 2½ feet apart

Four beanbags

Administrators:

One director

Two assistants

One scorer

Number of trials:

Three trials at each target

Directions:

"Do you see the red dot? (point out) I want you to hit the red dot with the beanbag. Throw them like this. Now you try to throw them like I did, and hit the red dot. What color is the next dot? Hit the blue dot. What color is the next dot after the blue? Hit the white dot. What color is the last dot? Can you hit the red dot?"

Scoring:

Composite number of throws contacting the targets

SOCCER KICK

Equipment:
    Three soccer balls
    One small rope
    Starting line
    Dimensional measuring area

Administrators:
    One director
    Two assistants
    One scorer

Number of trials:
    Three trials

Directions:
    "Can you kick a ball? Do you think you could kick this ball to Miss White? Watch me. Now will you try to kick it just like I did, and kick it very hard."

Scoring:
    Distance of the carry in feet

THROW—DISTANCE

Equipment:
    Three tennis balls
    Dimensional measuring area
    One set of footprints

Administrators:
    One director
    Two assistants
    One scorer

Number of trials:
    Three trials

Directions:
    "I want you to throw this ball. Throw it as far as you can. Do you think you can throw it over the fence?"

Scoring:
    Distance of the carry in feet

JUMP FROM HEIGHT

Equipment:
    A stably constructed height of 18 inches

Mat (optional)

Administrators:
    One director
    One scorer

Number of trials:
    Three sequential trials

Directions:
    "This makes you very tall doesn't it? Almost as tall as Miss White. Do you think you can jump down? Watch how I do it. Now you do just what I did. Are you ready? Jump."

Scoring:
    4 Points—Superior
    3 Points—Well defined
    2 Points—Modified
    1 Point —Poor
    0 Point —Not at all

BROAD JUMP (STANDING)

Equipment:
    A mat 72 inches long, marked with dimensions of 1 inch
    One yardstick

Administrators:
    One director
    One assistant
    One scorer

Number of trials:
    Three sequential trials

Directions:
    "See those footprints? I want you to stand on them. Can you see the cat? The dog? Do you think you can jump to the dog? Watch me. Now jump just like I did, and jump as far as you can. Ready, jump!"

Scoring:
    Distance in inches. Best of three trials recorded.

JUMP AND REACH (VERTICAL JUMP)

Equipment:
    Measuring device with 1-inch graduations (movable arm)
    One set of footprints

Administrators:
    One director
    One assistant
    One scorer
Number of trials:
    Three trials
Directions:
    "See those footprints? Can you stand on them? Now, see if you can *reach* the yellow. Now jump and see if you can *hit* the yellow spot. Jump as high as you can."
Scoring:
    Height in inches. Obtained by subtracting height of reach from height attained with jump. Best score recorded.

SHUTTLE SPRINT

Equipment:
    Two stopwatches
    Postman replica
    Letters (twenty-four)
    One set footprints
    One clothes pin
Administrators:
    One director
    One assistant
    One timer
Number of trials:
    One trial

Directions:

"Can you guess who that man is over there? Do you have a postman? Do you ever get a letter? Do you ever give the postman a letter to mail? Can you run very fast? I want you to run very fast to the postman and get the letter and bring it back to Miss White as fast as you can. Do you think you can do that? All right, run to the postman, get the letter, and bring it back to Miss White. Run as fast as you can. Ready, run!"

Scoring:

Number of seconds. Time starts at child's first movement, and ends as child crosses finish line.

CLIMB—LADDER

Equipment:

One six-run ladder

Administrators:

One director

One assistant

Two scorers

Number of trials:

One trial

Directions:

"Stand on the footprints. Now I want you to climb the ladder to the top, touch my hand, and go back down as fast as you can. Ready, climb."

Scoring:

Number of seconds. Time begins as hands touch ladder, and ends as one foot touches ground.

CLIMB—STEPS

Equipment:

Six stably erected steps

Administrators:

One director

One assistant

Three scorers

Number of trials:

One trial

Directions:

"Stand in the footprints. I want you to walk up the steps, and walk down the steps. Walk as fast as you can."

Scoring:

Number of seconds. Time begins as foot touches first step, and ends as one foot touches ground.

BALANCE BOARD—LOW

Equipment:

One 10-foot board (1 by 9 inches)

Administrators:

One director

One assistant

Two scorers

Number of trials:

One trial

Directions:

"I want you to walk across this board to Miss White. I want you to walk a new way. Watch me. Touch your heel to your toe each time you step. This is a different way isn't it? Do you think you can do it? All right, be sure to touch your heel to your toe each time you step."

Scoring:

4 Points—Superior

3 Points—Well defined

2 Points—Modified

1 Point —Poor

0 Point —Not at all

BALANCE BOARD—HIGH

Equipment:

One 10-foot board (1 by 9 inches)

Two bucks (24 inches)

Administrators:

One director

Three scorers

Number of trials:

One trial

Directions:

"How tall you are! I want you to walk across this board to Miss White. I want you to try to walk quickly."

Scoring:
   4 Points—Superior
   3 Points—Well defined
   2 Points—Modified
   1 Point —Poor
   0 Point —Not at all

Index